What I'd Teach Your Horse
Training & Re-Training the Basics

"What I'd Teach Your Horse" by Keith Hosman

ISBN-13: 978-1497496811
ISBN-10: 1497496810

Copyright 2012 Keith Hosman, First Edition
Copyright 2014-2016 Keith Hosman, Second Edition

All rights reserved. No part of this publication may be reproduced, stored in a retrieval system, or transmitted, in any form or by any means, electronic, mechanical photocopying, recording, or otherwise, without the prior written permission of the publisher.

Please note: The information appearing in this publication is presented for educational purposes only. In no case shall the publishers or authors be held responsible for any use readers may choose to make, or not to make, of this information.

Keith Hosman
horsemanship101.com
PO Box 31
Utopia, TX 78884 USA

033116 2.1

Horse Training How-To from Horsemanship101.com

What I'd Teach Your Horse
Training & Re-Training the Basics

Second Edition

Keith Hosman, John Lyons Certified Trainer

Part of the "Horse Training How-To" Series from Horsemanship101.com
Find step-by-step horse training articles 24/7 at Horsemanship101.com/Articles

Contents

Preface 11

Section I
Basically training your horse

Legs Mean Move 15
(Step 1 if This Is "Day 2" for Your Young Horse) Your young and very green horse has learned to pack a saddle and you've sat on it once or twice—but you'd like to do something more than sit there and wave at your friends as they ride off. You want a horse that... moves. Here's what to do.

Hip Control, Part I 22
Control of your horse's hips is the key to all the "stuff your horse can do." Here we start unlocking your horse's potential with a few basic and easy exercises.

Hip Control, Part II 31
Our next objective is to better the horse's ability to move its hips on request, giving us not just a step or two, but a pivot over his shoulder of a full 180 degrees.

Classic Serpentine 37
The Swiss Army knife of training exercises, use this routine to warm up, cool down, lower your horse's head, connect the rein to the feet, or to soften laterally.

Train Your Horse to Travel Straight 41
Training your horse to walk, trot or lope in a straight line is easy. Here's how to do it.

Clockwork: Teach Anything to Your Horse 46
Here's a great primer for all future training: In the same way that you can use a hammer and saw to build a penthouse, doghouse or outhouse, you can use the "Clockwork Exercise" described here to teach your horse almost anything. Beyond teaching simple cues to "turn left" or "turn right," you can pick the appropriate numbers and teach a spin, a back up, a side pass... the options are endless.

Shoulder Control 49
How do you know when you know you've got no "shoulder control"? Four seconds before your knee hits a tree. Here we get the back half of your horse lined up squarely behind the front half. We'll fine tune your steering and get the two of you in shape for the more complex work you'll face when your horse graduates from basic training to graduate school, prepping it for a life as a reiner, eventer—or real cool, pushbutton trail horse.

The Reverse Arc Circle 58
We'll quickly teach the "reverse arc circle" as an example of how to get more advanced shoulder movement using "clock work." "Reverse Arc Circle" is a fancy way of saying "your horse looks off to one side, but pivots on his back foot going the other way," (he looks left, spins right). It's a first step to teaching the reining spin or neck reining.

How to Fix Leaning Shoulders 61
If your horse leans over or "drops a shoulder" in a turn, here's how to fix it.

Serpentine: Indirect to Direct 66
Here's an additional exercise that'll teach your horse to stay "upright" through his travels and put an end to "corner cutting."

Speed Control

Basic Speed Control..69
Presently, your horse knows just two speeds: "Slow" going away from the barn and "fast" going toward it. Here we teach it to slow down and speed up when lightly cued—but also to travel consistently at a wide range of speeds.

Slow Down, Part I: Move the Hip..76
If you have problems with your horse getting "higher and higher"—or need ways to slow a fast one down—then the following two sections are for you.

Slow Down, Part II: Wherein We Train the Brain.............79
When you want to teach your horse to slow down, a simple key is to find a moment when traveling on a loose rein and build on it.

Balky Horses: Comatose One Minute, Hot to Trot the Next...83
Here's what to do when your horse moves slower and slower on the way out of the barn—but faster and faster when headed toward it. Plus: The horse that won't move.

Crossing Creeks and Scary Stuff 88
Forcing your horse across obstacles without proper training is inviting trouble. Here's how to properly prepare your horse to walk across scary objects like tarps and water and to avoid fights. It's also great pre-training for teaching your horse to load into a trailer.

Teach Your Horse to Lower Its Head While Standing..97
"Horse, quit playing games with that appaloosa and behave yourself. Drop your head, leave it there, quit antagonizing me."

Better Back Ups **105**
If you've practiced the "Clockwork Exercise," specifically and successfully teaching your horse to step on "6 o'clock" repeatedly, then your horse can and will back up for you today. What we'll do here then is work to make the movement smoother and quicker.

Simple Steps to Power Steering **110**
We'll use what you learned in the Clockwork Exercise to firmly ingrain in your brain the importance of being specific with your requests—and we'll see how that precision can be used to turn on a dime and ride circles that don't look like eggs.

Diagonal Movement ("Leg Yields Without the Legs") **115**
What you'll achieve here: Smooth and easy diagonal lines of travel plus a "polite" horse that moves fluidly from a walk to a trot to a canter on the lightest of cues. What you'll fix: Horses that want to leap into and speed through their transitions, horses that ignore our cues, horses that just trod along "going through the motions."

Softening **124**
Get your horse giving to the bit, dropping its head and rounding its body, rather than bracing when you pick up the reins. Being "rounded" is the crux of collection. Collection gives us a horse that can readily follow our requests with lightness and precision with zero hesitation.

Getting Leads **135**
Teaching any horse to pick up the correct lead is ninety percent "softening" through its transitions. The rest is "positioning."

A Fix for Cross-Firing (aka "Cross-Cantering") **139**
Q: "How do I fix cross-firing in the lope? How do I even know when it's happening?

Hips, Get Behind the Shoulders (And Stay Put) 142
A little exercise with big results. Teach your horse to automatically align its hips and shoulders in an arc mirroring your line of travel to improve collection and see the following: 1) Rounder circles; 2) Straighter straights; 3) Vastly improved stops. (Oh! And it cures rubber necking!)

Hips-in (aka "Haunches-in" or "Travers") 146
Hips-in is strength training for your horse, a trip to the gym. It asks your horse to "more fully engage" the back inside leg and thus develop a greater ability to "round up" and carry you in a more energized and balanced frame. In turn, you get a more obedient horse that does anything that requires a sudden burst of power, better. (Like sharp turns, standing-start lope departures, pivots, and rollbacks.)

Neck Reining How-To 153
Teaching your horse to neck rein is simple—and here's how.

Section II
Teaching you, the theory behind the practice

The First Thing I Do 165
Here's the first thing you should do with your horse today—and with any horse that's "new to you."

Each Time You Mount Up, Do This 171
Here's one small thing you can do to keep your horse's attitude in check—and prevent mount-up problems from taking root.

How to Pick Up Your Reins Like a Pro 174
It is critical that you become practiced with your hands, your primary source of communication. This is—in detail—how to pick up, handle, and release your reins.

Training Magic: Release on the Thought....... 182
Two days from now your friends at the barn will be pointing at you excitedly, stepping from your path reverently and cooing "oooh" as they watch you ride.

What You're Feeling For 188
Just as another person might reach out a hand to shake yours as you approach, a trained horse will proactively read your body language and act, never waiting for a tug on the reins.

Reins Tell Direction, Legs Tell Speed............. 190
Is your horse getting duller to your cues? Do you make a request only to have him shoot you a condescending glance and go back to what he was doing? It might be that you're burning out your cues when you use them as both a "heads-up" and motivator.

Talking Horse... 193
Wouldn't it be cool if your horse spoke English and you could simply tell him what you were looking for when you're riding? Well, ta-da! Here's a trick to get your point across clearly, a technique that's simple and easy to remember.

See Yourself Leading When Riding................ 196
I'm going to give you a training technique you can use in the saddle, one simple change you can make today that'll make big—very cool—changes immediately. Your horse will understand your requests far more quickly and all it takes is for you to "see things differently."

Perfect the First Time 199
If you're guilty of being a bit heavy-handed (as evidenced by a stiff-as-a-statue horse) here's a Top Five training concept that will soften your horse very quickly.

Six Easy Ways to Improve Your Training........ 202
Here find six horse training tips, each designed to simplify your training and make big changes fast.

Rider Checklists 208
Here are 3 "Rider Checklists." Together, they'll keep you safer—and accelerate your training to boot.

Diagnosing Problems.. 216
Do you want your horse to stop doing something? Or to start doing something? Either way, the solution lies in asking yourself "What cue or cues plural is my horse ignoring?"

Books by This Author 218
Check out these titles from Keith Hosman

Meet the Author... 219
Keith Hosman, John Lyons Certified Trainer

Preface

If I had a dollar for every email I get asking "what to do" to make a riding horse out of the mare Uncle Emo just traded for the old RV—or how to retrain a horse that's grown rusty—or some version on either theme, I'd be the world's first gazillionaire. With the publication of this book then, I'm hoping to grab that distinction.

If you broke your horse to saddle and got on it for the first time yesterday, this book (chapter 1) is where you'd start tomorrow. If you have an older horse and you've taught him everything you know and he still don't know nothin', this book is where you'd start, (chapter 2). It's a road map to building the foundation every horse needs, regardless of age, breed or background, regardless of what you've got ultimately planned for that horse.

Afterward, when your horse knows this book back to front, go train for barrels, roping, eventing, jumping or dressage. But today, basics are basics.

Section I is the stuff your horse needs to know. Section II is the stuff (the theory) you need to know. Practice the first handful of chapters in order, as written. Beyond that, you should feel free to mix and match depending on your needs or abilities. Some chapters are dependent upon others—but in those cases, I've spelled out necessary prerequisites.

Keith Hosman
John Lyons Certified Trainer
Utopia, Texas

Section I

Basically training your horse

Legs Mean Move

(Step 1 if This Is "Day 2" for Your Young Horse) Your young and very green horse has learned to pack a saddle and you've sat on it once or twice—but you'd like to do something more than sit there and wave at your friends as they ride off. You want a horse that... moves. Here's what to do.

If the only experience your horse has with you as a rider is you strapping on a saddle then climbing up there and sitting, then the logical next step is to teach cues for movement. You'll take up your training with this chapter. If your horse is beyond such basics, skip ahead; begin your training in the next chapter.

Here we'll assume that you're breaking a young, green horse who has become accustomed to carrying a saddle around and to you climbing on and off at least fifty times.

With a horse in such an early, early stage of training, we will not initially use our legs to ask for movement. Kicking a young, scared horse is a certain ticket to a bucking adventure. Nor will we cue the horse in the beginning with a kiss for two reasons: 1) We don't (yet) have a way to force the horse to move if we kiss and it just stands there; we haven't made the connection in the horse's mind between the rein and moving his legs. If it ignores our cue and then we can't get the feet moving, we've taught it that the cue means nothing. 2) Horses at this stage are often looking for things to be scared of—you don't want to do anything that might unnecessarily startle the horse and cause a wreck. Instead, we'll use our reins, then slowly mix in our cues and motivators, our kisses and bumps.

Begin by asking your horse to keep his head off to the side by several inches: Pick up one rein and take your horse's head to the side, let's say to the left, then let go of the rein. (See the chapter "How to Pick Up Your Reins Like a Pro" for tips on rein handling, specifically the section on "one-handed rein exercises") When the horse brings his head back forward, pick up your rein and bring his head back to the left, releasing again when he does. It is important to understand that you are not holding his head in place with constant pressure. You are to drop your rein each time his head moves to the side. Why? Because if you pulled his head over and locked it there, he might feel trapped and react in kind. But also because if your horse begins to associate his movement with your pressure on the reins, it will always require pressure to get the horse to move. We want the horse to move with no pressure on the reins.

In time, your horse will tire of having his head off to one side and he'll move his body to line up, in effect "straightening" his neck. He'll move his hips to the right if you'd picked up the left rein and vice versa. Repeat this sequence until the horse realizes that you will allow him to keep his head forward when he moves his feet.

Keep your gestures simple, calm and fluid—far, far away from "reprimanding or demanding." But, don't be so calm that your horse forgets you're there. You want to stay active. You don't want to sit quietly for a bit then reach for the rein only to have the horse realize with a start that something's on his back. Actively work to keep your existence remembered. You can talk to the horse so he can hear you, you can change your posture, you can adjust the reins—don't let the horse forget you're there. (And if you want to pet your horse, let'm know it's coming: Lightly tap the saddle, then tap the edge of the saddle, then tap the horse near the saddle... work your way out toward it's head or back end. Suddenly reaching back and patting that backside will get you launched.)

While the horse might move any or all of his four feet to start, what you'll likely notice is that he'll most often move his back end to do the "lining up," it's only logical. Let's use that; let's start getting specific responses to very specific requests. In your mind, place a one inch dot anywhere on your horse's left hip and then on its right hip. (Better yet, get a cattle marker and make your marks for real.) Now you will concentrate solely on moving those dots to their left or right.

Start each sequence by saying out loud to the horse "Move the dot on your left hip to the left" or "Move the dot on your right hip to the right." As you've seen, the left rein will cause the hips to move to their right, the right rein causes them to move left. Practice that now: Pick up your left rein, concentrate on the right dot, say "move right." Bring the horse's head to its left and insist that it keep its head to the side until it moves that dot in the chosen direction (to the right, in this example) to any small degree. Repeat and practice in both directions.

(Here's another good reason to start with the back legs: If your horse were to start bucking or to lurch unexpectedly, you would want to react by bringing its hips over, lessening the driving power it can put into each hop. Getting control over that back end, then, is a smart first move on your part.)

When your horse will reliably move it's hips (and, hence, its back feet) to both the right and left, change your focus to the front feet. Place your "dots" on the left and right shoulders. Follow the same thinking and pattern, except this time use the rein on the same side as the dot you'd like to see move, (a "direct rein"). Say out loud "move the dot on your right shoulder to the right," then pick up the right rein and bring the head to the side and release. Keep bringing the head back to the side and concentrating on your dot until it moves to the side (not forward, not backward, but to the side). If the horse stalls out at anytime, get the back feet to move. Don't allow it, if at all possible, to start hanging on that rein. By contrast, the other three dots you've placed might move (and move and move)—but just ignore that until your chosen dot moves correctly. Only then release.

Practice moving the shoulders and hips-in a myriad of combinations and in a short while, what you'll find is that the horse simply stays moving. He might do this because he finds walking easier than a constant barrage of requests from you to move this shoulder, then that hip, but regardless, now you have a way to cause the horse to move.

As you ride, don't try to steer. Any amount of rein handling causes the horse to slow, so just meander and only use your reins to get the horse moving. Do what you gotta do to keep the horse moving out fluidly. See yourself as the fans in the stands at a baseball game, working to keep a giant beach ball in constant play above their heads.

When you can dependably get both the shoulders and the hips to move with your rein, begin teaching the "kiss cue" and the "leg bump motivator." First, get your horse moving. Then, AFTER moving a few steps, kiss. Move... kiss. Bring the horse to a stop by asking the hips to step to the side. Practice just that sequence, kissing to your horse only after it's already moving. Try not to go very far before bringing the horse to a stop. Traveling only short distances will help keep the horse's body more rounded and give you a bit more control if something should spook it. Were it to become startled, you'd want to bring the hips around to draw power from those back legs. If the body was rock solid straight (and the horse pointed directly forward), he'd be in a better position to push through anything you might do to bring him back under control

Next, add the leg bump: Ask the horse to move and kiss to it after a few strides. Seconds later, bump lightly with both legs. Travel a few more beats, then bring the hips around to stop. Again, practice this sequence, first getting movement, then kissing, next bumping, stop with a turn of the hips. When your horse has become accustomed to your kiss and leg bumps as it travels, begin kissing then bumping just as your horse moves off.

Next, introduce the "kiss and bump" from a standstill. Remember that a kiss is a cue (it asks for something) while your legs apply motivation (they say "Hey, you missed that kiss. Move now or I'll irritate you with this incessant thump, thump, thump"). From a stand still, pick up and move your reins forward (a sort of "pre-cue") and kiss. If the horse doesn't move forward, bump. If the horse doesn't move off the bump, then use your reins to bring the back legs around or step the front legs across. Do something to get movement—do not let the horse learn to ignore your requests. In short order, your horse will begin moving off your kiss to avoid the bump he learns is sure to follow.

Finally, add the following to your sequence: When you kiss to initiate movement, simultaneously drop your legs against the horse, wrapping them briefly around the barrel with the weight of two wet towels. One half-second after making contact, let your legs fall back away, carried away by gravity. Follow this with a bump only if the horse ignores your kiss cue.

Throughout training sessions that follow, work on solidifying the sequence described. Beyond your horse's training, you need to really drill on the pattern, creating muscle memory for you the rider. Pick up the reins, kiss, wrap your legs, allow your legs to fall away. Bump if ya gotta. Later in your horse's career, the "wrapping legs" will act as a pre-cue, signaling to him that he needs to round his body and "collect up." The more heads-up you give the horse, the more natural and correct his movements will be.

Your job here, as you prep for later days and more advanced work, is to teach the horse to think forward, to move with an even cadence, and to keep moving until "I say otherwise." Begin by teaching the sequence: "I pick up the reins, kiss, and briefly round up my legs and you move off. I bump if you miss the cue to move." Keep the horse moving smoothly. Don't stop at fences or to sniff the backsides of other horses. Find an even rhythm in your gait and work to maintain that flow. Don't be thrown by the horse nearing fences, other horses or any other immovable objects. If he slows, time your thumping to keep him moving. If you allow him to approach a fence in his wanderings and stop just two times, he'll start looking for fences like a dog hunting rabbits. If he's pointed straight at a fence, keep thumping till he moves. Keep him moving and you'll soon be in a position for more advanced work. (And always return to an earlier point in your training anytime your horse becomes unduly anxious or otherwise slow to learn.)

Hip Control, Part I

Control of your horse's hips is the key to all the "stuff your horse can do." Here we start unlocking your horse's potential with a few basic and easy exercises.

The ability to control your horse's hips is paramount in any training program. It's where we begin training the green horse, the key you'll need to unlock "stuff your horse can do." Stuff like turning; that's an obvious example. (Turn the hips, turn the horse.) But hip control is also critical to gaining shoulder control in the early stages of training and to more advanced maneuvers later on such as the flying lead change or correcting dropped shoulders. Vital to schooling the young, sometimes-rambunctious green horse, it also lends the ability to shut your bronc down when it gains too much speed or to force a change of direction when he's thinking left and you're thinking right.

We'll begin with a quick ground lesson before getting you into the saddle.

Put a headstall, reins and snaffle bit on your horse. (You don't want to start this work using a halter. The signal to the horse isn't as clear as from the bit and some horses who are especially out of control can drag you from here to eternity if they're simply outfitted in a halter.) You'll also need a dressage whip.

Do this exercise with a friend—you'd be surprised what they can see from their vantage point. Their insight and honesty might speed you through this.

Flip the reins over the horse's neck as if you're going to ride. Stand on his left side, near his shoulder, facing him. Take the rein near his mouth just below the slobber strap so that your thumb is toward the rear of the horse. Raise the dressage whip in your right hand as if conducting the Philharmonic and kiss. If he doesn't move (and he probably won't at first), tap him on the rump. If he still doesn't move, relax, you gotta start somewhere. You can tap a little harder, perhaps quicker in order to "kind of annoy" the horse. Don't smack the horse unless you're willing to chance a quick kick to your ribs. Trust me, you'd be amazed how high and far those back legs can reach.

Keep tapping, annoying the horse till it moves; teach him that your body language (raising the whip, for instance) means move forward.

Apply a little "back" pressure with your left hand on the rein—but ask the horse (with your crop and stance) to move forward. He'll have little choice, if you're persistent, than to bend his neck a little. That's what you're looking for: a little give. Release immediately. Skip this step and you'll find that some horses will simply go straight up on their hindquarters (dragging you with them) as the training progresses. So, don't.

Next step: Without your horse, look down at the ground and slowly spin around, being careful to keep your feet within the same 1 square foot of ground. You should be simply turning around in the same spot like the center of a clock. Put your hands out like you're conducting again, your baton, sorry, crop, in your right hand. Pretend a horse is there, traveling around you like the Earth around the Sun.

Staying in one spot is important; horses think like this: "I'm the boss if I can make you move—and vice versa." And we're trying to gain control—so listen up, this is important. Remember that great line in "A League of Their Own" when Jon Lovitz says to the girl "See, how it works is the train moves, not the station." Same thing here: While you may get dragged when you first begin, try your best to stay in one spot as you conduct this training and your horse walks around you.

Now, get your horse and do the same thing: With the rein in the left hand (as before) and your crop at the ready, ask your horse to walk around you in a circle to the left. Look down and watch the horse's front and back feet. What we want is for the horse to travel around you with the back and front feet on the same track even briefly. If the horse's shoulder is too far away and the hips too close (as if the horse is looking or turning to the right and pulling you along) then take a step back and pull the horse's head with you. If the shoulder is too close (and the hip too far), then simply step away; at this point in your horse's training we have little choice but to get out of the way. In either case, try speeding the horse up to bring him more into line, being careful to guide that oncoming shoulder away from you as best you can, smoothly around to the left.

If the horse turns in to you and tries to stop... don't let him. Immediately get him moving again, in essence saying "That is not what's going to get you a release. Get moving." You may have to do this quite a few times before your horse learns the mechanics. Be firm and quick about it. Your biggest enemy is the horse losing momentum and rocking back.

At first, turn with your horse. But, the moment your horse takes that second consecutive step with both front and back feet on the same set of tracks, stop spinning but ask the horse to continue walking around you for two steps. (You'll stop, he won't.)

Smoothly step out and bring the horse's nose toward his rear, causing the hips to swing around (to your left if you're standing on the side from which you typically lead and later vice-versa). When you first begin you may need to really try and make the nose touch the hip. Not literally possible, sure, but thinking you are will help. Keep the back legs rotating around the front of the horse until the horse's inside front leg (the one nearest you) stops, however briefly. Walk the horse forward a few steps and release all pressure. Done.

Pitfall: Don't allow your horse to lose its motion and rock back. If he just kind of mulls around, put some energy into him with your trusty dressage whip. Horse and human should always be thinking "forward." The most important thing your horse is going to gain out of this whole exercise is his making the connection between pressure on his mouth (via the rein) and your request to move his hips. To get that you'll need forward motion. Lots of it. A nice side effect of this exercise, by the way, is that it has a nice way of softening your horse's neck—that is, as long as you are kind, patient, and release the moment the horse even thinks about taking the correct step.

Do the exercise as described above on the left side then release the reins, move to the front of the horse and pause to pet him (the pause-to-pet part is very important). Then move to the right side and repeat. Move back and forth between each side of the horse after each repetition. You'll find the horse more agreeable, more supple, on one side than the other. Stick with it and, in due time, the "flexibility" evens out.

Always release as soon as possible—but if your horse wants to lean back toward the end of this movement (sort of pulling on your arm) then keep the pressure and immediately get him moving forward and around again—as if to say "You didn't do it right so you're going to keep moving." Don't, whatever you do, give the horse a chance to "park" himself there, pulling back on the bit. That will haunt you later.

The entire time you're doing this work you should be seeing yourself on the horse's back—after all that's our goal, to get you riding safely. It's important now to see yourself up there, picturing what it'll take later to get these same movements.

You're done with this exercise (from the ground) when your horse will lightly stop his shoulder and move his hips around obligingly each and every time you ask.

This sort of movement is called a "disengagement" because that's what it does: It takes the power from one leg and gives it to the other. If you yourself were to sidestep to the left, the left leg is engaged, the right is being pulled and therefore is disengaged. When horses "disengage" several things happen: the back feet move a little closer to the front, the horse becomes a bit "off balance" and, virtually by definition, the horse slows down, handing you more control.

What you undoubtedly found while doing that ground work, was that the more smoothly or fluidly you kept both the horse's feet and your own hands moving, the better your results tended to be. Picture a ballerina. Her dance sequence isn't full of fitful stops and starts. She moves fluidly and, here's the key, she moves at the same tempo regardless of whether she's moving forward or backward—or transitioning from moving forward to moving backward. Likewise, you should concentrate on keeping your horse's feet moving at the same tempo, like that dancer, regardless of the steps called for in your "routine."

Now from the saddle, we're going to teach our horse to move his hips over just as you did on the ground (though at first we'll only ask for a step or two). However, you're going to use a trick to cause this to happen a bit quicker. Mount up now and walk to the nearest wall or fence line. Walk with the fence on your left and picture the horse stepping his hips off to the right by about twelve inches in response to your picking up the left rein. Once pictured, go ahead and give it a try: Pick up and apply pressure to the left rein, just enough to put a very slight bend in his neck. Pause a few seconds, walking and waiting. When he ignores your cue to move his hips over (because this is the first time you've practiced this) apply more pressure, enough to turn his entire body perpendicular to the fence—as if turning back the other way. You may stop briefly here (with his nose to the fence) because of the dramatic change in positioning—and that's fine—but use the right rein then to ask him to resume walking the same, initial, direction, (the fence on your left). Always pick up your rein and ask first with the lightest of pressure before applying more "motivation" should he miss your initial request. Remember, "he'll only ever be as light as the lightest pressure you use."

Here's a tip: Just as on the ground, you will find that bringing the rein to your opposite shoulder (or "where the saddle horn would be") will work on one side, pulling the rein toward the horse's hip will work on the other side.

Repeat that sequence. Walking with the fence to your left, think "move your hips to the right" and apply pressure to the left rein. If and when he ignores your cue, pull hard enough a beat later to turn him wholly perpendicular to the fence. The simple initial pressure you apply is your cue, applying increasing pressure, enough to actually turn him, is motivation. It "motivates" him to figure out what gets you out of his mouth: Stopping and turning his entire body is hard work, so he'll soon learn that he can save himself the effort by simply jutting his hip over to the right.

Note: It is critical that when you do ask the horse to turn, that you do it with the attitude that you really are going to turn back and go the other way. Don't think "turn to the fence." Think "turn and go back the other way"—then simply stop your horse when he's perpendicular. If you don't carry this thought, you'll find yourself just sort of slogging around, aimless.

Bear in mind that we're not looking for him to move his hips over more than about twelve inches (thirty degrees, give or take)—and that's not all that much. You're "breaking the ice," "giving him the idea." If you have trouble "seeing how this feels," lay a rope parallel to the fence, separated by the width of your horse plus a foot or two. You'll then have two paths, the one you've been traveling, there near the wall, the second marked by the rope. Walk your horse along the wall and ask the back legs (only) to move over (doing so as already described) and touch the rope before returning to their original path along the wall. That's it. That quick back and forth (cha cha cha!) sideways movement of the hips is all we're looking for.

When you believe you've got the feel for this, move away from the wall (your "crutch") and ask a friend to watch you, the friend barking out "yes" or "no." Yes, you moved the hips over briefly onto a second path while the front feet stayed on the original path—or no, you're just turning. (If your horse was a car traveling in the left "passing" lane, his back legs would step briefly across into the right lane and then back again when done correctly. Incorrect would be your horse (the car) turning from the left lane into oncoming traffic.) If shifting the hips over like this is new to you, do not forgo asking for your friend's help. Almost one hundred percent of the people learning to move the hips like this "think" it's happening when in fact, what they're doing is simply turning like that car, straight into oncoming traffic. You must, must, must, must learn to feel the difference. Know in advance that you, too, will make this mistake, so asking a friend to spot you (and confirm your actions) is mandatory. Do not move ahead until your friend gives you the thumbs up.

You'll discover that the horse rather quickly begins moving his hips over for a step or two when you simply reach for the reins. Practice this until the horse really "gets it," being sure to release the reins when you think the horse is even thinking of moving those hips over, turning him back toward the wall each time he ignores your request.

Be especially careful to keep moving and thinking forward, with no stops and starts in your "dancing." (Move up to a trot if you need to stoke a little energy.) Keeping fluid keeps all this energy channeled directly into training, eliminating many outside distractions. And, there's another reason: It helps develop your timing and "feel" for the reins. "Staying fluid" forces you to think ahead, to keep your angles wider, your pressure more even. In that way, you'll naturally divert or deflect the flow of the horse's energy and you can avoid setting up unnecessary confrontations. (You're equine partner will also begin trusting you more.)

Next, pick up a trot and nail this (you pick up a rein, he moves his hips over briefly) going both directions at the quicker gait. Ideally, you will advance in your training to the point that the horse doesn't actually stop and move his hips, instead he continues moving forward as he bring the hips over for a moment. When the two of you are solid at a trot, move away from the wall and practice there (at a walk, then trot).

Note: When you and your horse begin most exercises that are "new to you," teach yourself at a walk then teach the horse at a trot. You need the slower pace to put the puzzle together in your head and develop muscle memory. The horse needs the higher speed because it means higher repetitions—and because it keeps the energy up. Horses tend to shuffle around at a walk and are far more apt to be thrown off by any little diversion. Remember: At a walk, you learn the material, at a trot the horse learns the material.

Hip Control, Part II

Our next objective is to better the horse's ability to move its hips on request, giving us not just a step or two, but a pivot over his shoulder of a full 180 degrees.

Now from the saddle, you will mimic the work you did in the previous chapter from the ground: Mount up and walk off. Look down at the left shoulder of the horse. Do you see how it moves forward then backward with each step the horse takes? Lock that moving picture in your memory.

Next, check your horse's energy level: Is he moving out energetically—or does it feel like you're driving your car with the brakes on, like a car running out of gas? For the following, you MUST have energy in the horse so, if necessary, bump it up a notch to get it moving forward fluidly, readily.

Pick up a single rein, let's say the left one for this example. (Don't lean forward!) Stare at the movement of the left shoulder as you ask the hips to step sideways to their right as you've practiced previously from the ground, a "disengagement." When you feel the horse's hips move to the side, let go and walk forward.

At any point, did you see the shoulder stop while the hips continued to move, even for half a second? Was the shoulder planted like a post, the hips pivoting around that post? Yes? Great—that's what we want. The shoulder stops while the hips move. No? Then ask for repeated disengagements, staring at the shoulder and altering the way you hold your rein (the angle, the pressure), until you can cause that shoulder to stop (however briefly) while the hips are still moving. Recall how you made this happen on the ground, the timing, the angles, the pressure, the movements... and now make it happen from the horse's back. If you did it then, you can do it now. The very instant you see both happening at the same time, the shoulder stopped, the hips moving, let go and move forward. That is all you need to accomplish in this chapter. But it is very, very important for future training.

Move out. Pick up a single rein and ask for a disengagement. Play with the pressure and angles you use until you are able to cause the shoulder (on the same side as the rein you're holding) to stop while the hips continue to move. Release and walk out.

This is actually fairly easy if you're patient and don't over-think it. Your bumping and rein pressure say "move, just don't move forward." Note: If you pull his head around too awkwardly he'll most likely freeze up, too knotted to move. Patience plays a major role here. Give him time to find the correct step and release your rein quickly and consistently to say "That's it there."

When first learning this, most horses will just sort of scramble around, slowing, but never actually stopping that front shoulder. Don't be fooled. Your goal is to get the shoulder stopped while those back legs keep moving. Ya gotta get both for the horse to get his reward (which is your release of pressure). Think of it as placing an order at the local burger joint: They don't get your money till you get the burger AND fries, not one or the other. It's very important that you know now that you may only get both of these things happening together (a stopped shoulder with moving hind feet) for a brief moment, maybe literally half a second—but in the beginning that's great and you need to fully release your pressure. Build on that. Through practice you will gain the ability to pivot a full 360 (if you were in to such a thing—but that's overkill for this work).

Use one rein throughout this exercise. You'll pick up the left rein, let's say, and use it to A) bring his head around, B) stop the shoulder and, C) drive the hips over. While you may be tempted to use both left and right reins simply out of habit, know that pulling on both sides together will (in this case) cause the horse to resist, lining up his entire skeletal system like stacked bricks against your pressure. (And he can stay like that all day long with little effort.) Instead, use a single rein to encourage the horse to keep his body curved, banana-like. With his body rounded, however slightly, he'll be forced to use muscle to resist and he'll sooner rather than later begin relaxing to your requests because it's just plain easier. (See the chapter "How to Pick Up Your Reins Like a Pro," specifically the section marked "One-handed rein exercises," for help with your rein-handling skills.)

Here are a couple of suggestions if you're having trouble causing the horse's shoulder to stop and the back legs to step over. First, with your hands empty, take your left fist and reach up and tap your right shoulder. Tell your fist to remember that spot. Reverse that, touching your right fist to your left shoulder. Do this several times so as to remember where your shoulders are located. (Seems obvious, I know, but you'd be amazed how folks can't seem to find their shoulders when riding in a clinic.) Next, get your horse moving, take up the rein in your left hand, bringing it out and away from the horse by about a foot and bring it back around in a smooth arc towards your opposite (that is, your right) shoulder. You'll be outlining a very large and rounded "check mark" with your fist in the air. Be very careful to make this movement in a giant arc, no sharp angles. (This means you.) In the end, your fist won't actually touch your shoulder—but it needs to be headed in that direction and it may come pretty close. Also, I often see riders at this point that really should be gripping the reins closer to the horse's mouth, so ask yourself if that might not help you out as well.

Because of the way horses tend to naturally carry themselves, bringing your hand out and around to your shoulder (the "check mark" move) will work on one side—but on his opposite side you'll probably find that you'll need to direct your pressure not toward your opposite shoulder but toward the horse's own butt on the same side. (So your hand will simply reach down and "pull" the horse's head directly toward his rear end.) Use two hands if you have to, but really make that horse think he's about to kiss his own hiney. Experiment to find out which method (check mark or hiney kiss) works for which side. Remember to keep your balance and to drop the reins (living to fight another day) if you feel the horse becoming unbalanced to the point that he might actually trip over his own feet.

If you're having trouble understanding what it feels like in that moment when the shoulder is stopped and the back legs are pivoting, ask a friend to watch. Have them watch and call out to you when to release. (You don't decide. You hold your pressure until they tell you to let go based on what they're seeing from the ground.) After each repetition replay those last few seconds in your brain and memorize that feeling. Ask them to test you when you think you've got it. It'll "click for you" pretty quickly this way.

You may be having trouble remembering which way the hips are going to go when you pull this rein or that rein. Here's a simple way to forecast what'll happen: If you were just riding down the trail and pulled on the left rein, which way would his hips go? To the right, of course. Well, it's no different when you're looking for a disengagement to the right or left and need to quickly decide which rein to pull.

Finally, the most common issue I see is that riders often have trouble keeping their horses moving—and movement is critical to training. If you're riding a more laid-back or stubborn horse, he'll be looking for any reason to stop and park out. Be aware of this and be ready with your legs. You may need spurs or a crop. You maybe should also try asking for less out of your horse—and by that I mean try first getting him to relax and just sorta "go with the flow." Remember always that it's not the exercise that's hard—it's the resistance. If your horse is reacting to rein pressure by slowing down rather than softening, then make it your immediate goal to cause the horse to move and "give to the bit." Refer to the chapter covering the "Classic Serpentine" exercise: Walk a straight line and use direct-rein pressure to ask your horse to turn. Hold your pressure through that turn, waiting till your horse softens his neck muscles slightly and drop the rein. You'll do this within the turn itself. (Asking for "softness" while changing leg direction or speed just seems to help them remember things.) Grow your training from there, eradicating resistance not through brute force but by offering more of a partnership: "I won't jerk on the reins if you soften up." Practice often, remaining patient and adamant and you'll see marked improvement in no time.

Classic Serpentine

The Swiss Army knife of training exercises, use this routine to warm up, cool down, lower your horse's head, connect the rein to the feet, or to soften laterally.

Here's a great exercise that you can (or should) start out your training sessions with every day forever. It relaxes the horse's body and causes it to lower its head. It reinforces the essential connection between reins and feet and it improves your turns. It also gives you many opportunities in a short time frame to get the horse to practice saying yes, which betters overall control. It's a core exercise in your regimen for all of those reasons plus it's something you can use anytime you need to calm down—or warm up—your horse.

Every day of your life you must actively work to build and protect a direct link between your reins and your horse's feet. Don't ever pick up and place pressure on a rein if you don't want to see a change in direction or speed. If you inadvertently teach the horse that the reins mean nothing by picking them up several thousand times and asking for no change in either path or pace, then it's no wonder that you think left and it goes right. The steering wheel isn't connected to the wheels and you have no control. This exercise helps reinforce that connection, so while your doing it, it is very important that you only release your pressure on the reins when the horse SOFTENS AS HE'S TURNING, not when going straight forward.

Begin at a stand still with zero pressure on the reins. Ideally they'd be dropped, lying on the horse's neck.

Pick up the reins and move forward at either a walk or trot. It's your choice: At a walk you learn the exercise, at a trot the horse learns it. As you move, try your best to apply zero pressure to the horse's mouth. Look for a droop in the reins as proof of this.

When you're ready, ask the horse to turn by applying pressure on one rein or the other. For example, use your left hand to ask the horse to move in an arc to the left. Note that, while your left hand is asking for the turn by applying pressure to your horse's mouth, your right hand should also play an active role, "helping out" the left by pulling out or adding slack. In this example, if you continually find yourself holding the rein either too close to the horse's mouth or too far away (that is, you've got too much slack), then you're not using that right hand to help the left. Both hands MUST be active.

Consciously feel the pressure exerted by the horse's stiff neck on your left hand. When that pressure lessens—or the horse lowers its head however slightly—let go of the rein entirely and pet your horse. (Watch the tip of the horse's ear if you need something to focus on.)

Go forward exactly two steps. Not one, not three... two. Being objective keeps you focused and it keeps you proactive, not reactive. It also forces you to improve your coordination and timing. If you want to make it three, that's fine, but pick a number and stick with it.

Pick up the opposite rein, ask the horse to turn to the other way and repeat the process.

From there you'll simply meander around, left then right, right then left. Make sure that when you ask for a turn, that you don't release until the horse is actively turning AND giving. (It's simple; just keep the horse turning till he softens and release the instant he does.) That helps keep (or make) the connection in the horse's brain between the rein and the feet. Tip: Set your horse up for success. Don't turn too sharply.

Remember our perennial rule: The longer you hang on to the rein, the less you should release on. Meaning, the longer you hang on to the reins, the less picky you are, the less the horse has to do to get a release. If you're looking for the head to drop (just as an example), then you might be looking for a two inch drop in the first few seconds... but after getting nothing for, say, twenty seconds, you might let go on 1/8 of an inch.

If your horse develops a rubber neck (he simply throws his head way over to the left by your boot and leaves it there) resist the temptation to pull his head back with the opposite rein. Instead change your focus to the back of the horse, boost the entire horse forward with your legs, and find the angle or amount of pressure it takes to cause him to move his hip over, bringing his head back into alignment with his rear end. For example, if you're holding the left rein and he brings his head to your left boot, you'd cause the horse's hips to move to their right with that same left rein. It's more work for the horse to move the hips than to simply turn through his shoulders, so this should end the rubber necking. Don't get mad—horses that do this are usually just doing what they think you want. Teach them. (If "rubber necking" continues to be an issue, look to the upcoming chapter ("Serpentine: Indirect to Direct") for a stand-alone exercise designed to deal with this specifically.)

If you pick up the reins and you feel no softening or dropping of the neck and time is passing you by, (let's say more than 30 seconds), then simply change your focus to the hip and ask the hip to move over a step, (as above). Your attitude at this point should be "It doesn't matter to me if you soften your neck or drop your head—but you're gonna move your hips sideways if you don't." So, with each repetition in your serpentine pattern, you will pick up the rein, count off the seconds in your head and if the neck doesn't soften or drop 1% more than the time before, just change your focus and ask the hips to move over. Release the reins when the hips move even if the neck remains stiff and raised. With enough practice, asking the hips to move one way then the other will have the effect of softening your horse's neck muscles, giving you the chance to further refine things with your hands.

Concentrate throughout on ensuring that your horse is moving forward fluidly and evenly. Squeeze with both legs if you feel even a trace amount of hesitation (for instance, should you have to ask the hips to move). Also, be alert and careful to feel for the horse softening however slightly. Sometimes we start pulling so hard we don't realize that the horse couldn't relax even if he wanted to.

Practice this serpentine often and progress to doing it at the lope. It's a terrific way to calm the horse, dissolve resistance in the neck and lower the head, teach it to follow its nose—and reaffirm that when you pick up the rein, those feet need to change somehow. It's also great anytime you're out riding and need to remind your horse of your existence.

Train Your Horse to Travel Straight

Training your horse to walk, trot or lope in a straight line is easy. Here's how to do it.

In the world of horse training, there are a few tricks we humans can quickly and easily teach our horses: How to bang on the stall door at feeding time; how to run away at the sight of an advancing halter; how to dance when they see a saddle, and so on. But then, there's the simple stuff like, y'know, just walking in a darned straight line that they never seem to "get."

And it's important to train for "straight." You don't want to spend future rides with your horse veering off his line and you grabbing up the reins to course correct every few seconds any more than you want to constantly badger your horse to jog. It's "pick up a jog and stay jogging till I ask for something else" and "Walk straight, keep going straight."

Walking in a straight line, keeping collected as we trot, loping an upright and round circle, reining spins… these are all examples of the abstract shapes we place our horse into or expect them to follow. Problem is, they make no sense to the horse and he has a hard time remembering such odd directives with no connection to his reality. It'd be like insisting, with no explanation, that your sister walk with a repeated kick step like a Rockette when in your presence or that your dad always march like a tin soldier when he goes out to fetch the mail.

So how to train for a straight line? We can ask for a straight line and put the horse on one... but he'll keep coming off it until we've corrected it about 566,405 times. How do we motivate the horse to "stay where we put him" without it taking a million years?

By combining our requests with something that helps him remember, a motivator.

Teaching a horse to travel on its own (forward or backward) in a straight line is first a matter of teaching the horse to turn right and left, and then of motivating him to go where he's pointed with no further corrections. Motivation comes from teaching him that "straight" is easier than "not going straight." We do that by convincing the horse that he becomes invisible to us when he moves in a particular fashion. He moves straight and life is a picnic; he falls off our radar, so to speak. He turns incorrectly and suddenly he's "exposed" to more work. It doesn't take long before he starts trying to "hide from us" by assuming a certain (correct) stance or direction, sort of like the elephant Horton hiding behind the daisy.

Imagine a kid's toy boat. It's motorized, battery-powered and being propelled by the little spinning prop in the back. Your daughter, Jane, and your son, Bob, are in a pool, sending the boat back and forth to each other. To make it travel across to Bob, Jane points the boat toward him—but she does so by bringing the rear of the toy toward herself. That's an important idea. Picture that happening in your mind's eye: She brings the BACK of the boat toward herself to make the whole thing go toward her brother. The rear of the boat determines the path of the entire boat.

We'll keep that analogy in mind as we train our horse to follow a straight line. You'll turn your horse as Jane turned the boat. For two reasons. First: Asking the horse to sweep its hips across actually makes the horse turn distinctly and immediately. Turning it's head does not. You can look one way and walk the other and so can he – so why would he make a connection in his mind between you picking up the rein and him turning? You can turn the horse's head thousands of times before he learns to follow his nose with this feet. Using the tail to correct our course will, as we will see, cause the learning to happen much quicker. Second, such a large move supplies greater motivation. It's extra work for the horse to move his rear. If he's guilty of ignoring your requests, he'll soon realize it's far easier to just turn as you initially ask. Horse's hate being "put out" and quickly learn to follow the cue you first send when you pick up the rein, rather than waiting for you to force the issue by moving the hip.

Here's what you do: Lay a lasso or lunge line down on the ground and walk it. (Or, better, follow the shadow thrown by a nearby building or fence line.) Don't guide the horse with your reins; watch the ground. Your line offers instant, objective, and obvious proof: Are you walking straight ahead or not? Are both sets of (front and back) legs walking in the same track, yes or no?

Eventually, the horse will drift off your line. That's what you've been waiting for. Regardless of whether the front or the back of the horse steps away first, your fix is the same: Look directly ahead to the end of the line on which you were traveling and use the rein necessary to point the horse back in the correct direction. But here's the key: You want to very purposely "point your horse" as you would the boat, not by turning the head – but by turning the hips. Don't be at all concerned with how the horse carries itself; don't try to line up body parts, for instance, just focus on getting the hip turned and nothing else. Know that if you get the horse's engine (his hips) pushing you back onto your correct line of travel, the rest of the horse will line up all by itself, just as a trailer will always fall back in line with the cab of a truck.

When you first begin, concentrate on one thing: Getting the hip turned. Ignore completely the head carriage or any neck stiffness. With enough repetition, what you will find is that all the hip swinging actually causes the horse to lower its head and soften its neck. You might further encourage this phenomenon as the two of you progress by purposely releasing your rein when you feel the head or neck "give."

What will naturally happen when you first make a correction is that your horse will over-turn and you'll find yourself walking a wild zigzag pattern. You may want a turn of twelve degrees but your horse will turn a sharp forty-five. That's fine. Keep asking the hip to move, left then right, right then left, until the hip lands squarely behind you, driving you forward, back onto your chosen path. Then release your rein and walk on until your next "veering." It's all the mistakes the horse makes that show him "Oh, that's all you wanted, just walk straight. That's easy." What you'll find is that if you keep your mind clear and concentrate solely on turning the hip, your horse will get your message quicker; he'll begin traveling correctly on his own sooner. Depending on your horse's current level of training, it may take minutes, it may take weeks—but in the end, you'll find this "correction with the tail" method to be much quicker than the alternative of "pointing the head." Advance this maneuver by asking for softness and correct head elevation, then increase your speed to a trot and get your good responses there.

Clockwork: Teach Anything to Your Horse

Here's a great primer for all future training: In the same way that you can use a hammer and saw to build a penthouse, doghouse or outhouse, you can use the "Clockwork Exercise" described here to teach your horse almost anything. Beyond teaching simple cues to "turn left" or "turn right," you can pick the appropriate numbers and teach a spin, a back up, a side pass... the options are endless.

As you ride, look down at the ground and imagine four giant clocks, one under each of your horse's feet. Placing any foot onto twelve (on its own clock) is walking forward, onto six is backing up, etcetera. Were you to step off to the right, you'd be stepping onto one, two or three, (four or five if the step was diagonally back and to the right.) Keep in mind that three is stepping directly to the right and requires a full stop, however slight. Numbers four, five and six also require a slight stop followed by backward movement. Stepping repeatedly onto four gives you a spin to your right, a spin to your left requires lots of eights. Ask both the front and back foot to each step over and over again onto threes or nines and you've got a side pass.

Note that with "clock work," you primarily use one rein. Your left hand "calls the shots" while the right hand "helps out," feeding and taking up slack. Later your right hand carries the brunt of the work while the left hand helps out. If you find yourself forcing the horse into position using two hands, put one on your thigh to avoid the temptation of picking it up.

Doing this is simple to start: Pick up your right rein, stare at "three o'clock" on the ground under the front right foot and release the rein when your horse steps on the spot with the same foot. ("Three" is usually where I start because that direct-sideways step is pretty easy to get right off the bat.) Practice until you can consistently use the right rein to cause the right front foot to step onto "three." Then work on "four o'clock," "five o'clock," "six o'clock" and so on, all the way around.

Next, use the other rein to tell the same (the right front foot) to step consistently on all 12 numbers.

Then do the same thing with the other three legs. All twelve numbers. Both reins individually. You'll think this is impossible at first; you'll think some of the wild combinations simply can't be done, but it is, in fact, very doable if you work at it methodically. Stick with it—there's a very big payoff later when you're teaching some advanced maneuver that requires leg A, B, C, or D to be placed onto spot X, Y, or Z. Not only will you have that ability—but you'll have several ways to tell your horse to do it.

The training actually happens very quickly once the two of you get the idea: In your mind, pick a rein to use, a foot to move and a number on the clock to target. Then, pick up your rein and apply pressure, staring at a spot on the ground until the horse moves that foot onto that spot. With repetition, your horse learns which number you expect by reading your body language, by feeling your position in the saddle or weight in a particular stirrup, maybe the way you hold the reins. If you simply concentrate on a number and apply motivation, (that is, you keep pressure on the reins and occasionally bump with both legs to say "move") your horse will do the rest because he wants a release of pressure—and you'll keep him searching (you'll keep him moving) till he stumbles upon the correct answer. Your release says "That's what I want right there," it's a reward. Simply repeat this until the "number" and rein-to-foot combination is learned.

Be careful to make sure your horse truly knows to step onto a specific number when asked and that he does so without fail before asking for repeated steps onto that number—otherwise he'll associate your release with "just stepping," not stepping onto a particular spot. Getting greedy and pushing too fast is a major no-no and all too common. Take your time; don't fall into that trap. You'll anger your horse, get frustrated and improvement will lag or stall out completely. First prove to yourself that the horse really associates your requests with a specific spot on the ground. Verify this by picking totally random rein-foot-number combinations and noting his response.

Can you now see how you might use the Clockwork Exercise to easily teach any horse to back up or to spin or to side pass?

Shoulder Control

How do you know when you know you've got no "shoulder control"? Four seconds before your knee hits a tree. Here we get the back half of your horse lined up squarely behind the front half. We'll fine tune your steering and get the two of you in shape for the more complex work you'll face when your horse graduates from basic training to graduate school, prepping it for a life as a reiner, eventer—or real cool, pushbutton trail horse.

If your car's back tires were two inches out of alignment with its front tires, your circles and turns will be lopsided; your stops will be sloppy and choppy. You'd travel like a mad, drunken crab. The horse you ride might have similar issues so getting the front end lined up with the back end is a first step on the road to great steering and stopping. Line up one half of the horse with the other half of the horse, and bah-da-bing bah-da-boom, you got solid turns and true circles. (And from a dressage rider's point of view, you've fostered "throughness," that feeling that the energy generated by the back legs, that impulsion, is flowing freely through a relaxed, ready and willing horse.)

Shoulder control fixes crooked horses, making possible straight and true stops, circles, back ups, and lines of travel, but also allows you to open gates and avoid driving your knees into trees. Better still, it leads directly to more advanced maneuvers in later days. You can go on to teach your horse to:

- Pivot or turn on its rear legs
- Leg yield
- Side pass
- Neck rein
- Spin

The key to all of this: Softness. In this context it means "relaxed muscles, zero resistance." It means a horse that goes with the flow. Picture Frankenstein dancing Swan Lake—now picture Baryshnikov. Fluid vs. clunky, get the idea? This goes double as we work on shoulder control because, while we can "force the horse" to move his hindquarters when we turn his head far enough, getting those shoulders to step over cleanly takes finesse and far more thought on your part. He typically carries the bulk of his weight up there and he just ain't gonna move it if he don't wanna. Success in this arena requires that your horse not resist (the bit, specifically). From you, it takes timing and "feel." It means keeping the horse relaxed and for you to ask rather than tell.

FACT: When you force the horse to make a movement by ratcheting his head or some other body part into position with undue pressure, it will actually take you longer to teach the maneuver. When you concentrate instead on softness first and foremost, you'll find that the horse learns far, far more quickly.

When you can pick up the rein and the horse stays soft and continues moving out, you will find that you can also move his shoulders left or right easily, with very little pressure on the rein. How? Why? Because moving his shoulders is not hard for the horse; it's easy. What kept those shoulders from moving previously was the resistance.

What typically happens when you first begin working with a colt, (or any older horse set in its ways) is that you'll pick up a rein and the horse will slow his feet and brace against you. His natural reaction is to stiffen the muscles in his chin, head, and neck and lose all cadence in his movement. He doesn't know why he does it, he just does it. You pick up a rein, he fights it, and when he fights it, you don't get the movement you're looking for. Your job is to teach the horse that when you pick up a rein, he should keep his muscles relaxed and his feet moving at the same tempo, no changing his rhythm, no pulling on your hands. Get that, get your movement.

When you do the exercises that follow, know then that your objective is to move as lightly and evenly as a pair of ballroom dancers. (You and your horse, you're Fred and Ginger.) You want to be out there gliding about evenly even when changing directions. To reach that goal, you'll need to concentrate on squashing resistance (that is, stiff muscles and balky feet) wherever you find it and to do whatever it takes to keep moving at the same pace from the time you start moving until you stop moving. To see what I mean, walk across the room, spin on your heels and walk backward—but do not change the speed at which you move your feet at any point, particularly during the change-of-direction transition. Later, when you're riding and you pick up the reins or ask for some change in direction, DO WHATEVER IT TAKES to keep your tempo, no stutter steps, no hesitation. This might mean lessening your pressure or the angle at which you hold the rein, it might mean changing your timing or kicking harder.

It might mean taking a break for awhile or practicing something altogether different to reset things or get your head straight.

We'll break the ice with the following:

PART A: Warm up by practicing the serpentine exercise as described in the previous chapter ("Classic Serpentine") at a trot.

PART B: Now, practice that same serpentine, with the following additional instruction: As you ask the horse to turn using your left rein, apply pressure with that left rein and ask the horse to bring its chin in closer to an area just to the left of the center of its chest. (If your horse was wearing a bra, his chin would be approaching the left cup.) Release each time he softens or drops his head however slightly, trot forward, turn the other direction and try again. Practice on both sides until you can readily bring the chin to within 5 inches of his chest and the horse stays relaxed through this. It is vital that you do not bring it in much closer than that. Also note that, in this entire chapter, this paragraph is most critical to your success in moving the shoulders to their left or right. It's just that important.

PART C: Next spend quality time refreshing yourself and your horse on the Clockwork Exercise. Very specifically, spend your practice time stepping the right front foot onto "three" using your direct (that is, your right) rein. Then reverse that and practice stepping that left front foot onto "nine" using your left rein. Also, practice moving both front feet onto "three" and "nine"—but use your indirect rein, the left to move right, the right to move left. (You might also refer back to chapter 1, "Legs Mean Move," for a related discussion.)

PART D: We'll ask the horse to move its shoulders off an indirect rein. It'll be "looking one way but walking another." Ride out at a walk and find a nice long shadow along the ground. If you can't find a shadow, lay a rope down in a straight line or use a fence for guidance. Do the following: 1) Walk the line with your reins dropped on your horse's neck. 2) Pick up both reins. Apply just enough pressure to your left rein to cause the horse to cock his head two to four inches to the left and bring its chin toward its chest as you continue walking your line. 3) Being careful to keep the horse's head cocked to the left, take your right arm (and the right rein) way out to your right. 4) Look down and stare at a small spot on the right shoulder and ask it to move to its right by applying pressure to the outside rein (the right one in this instance) in the direction you'd like to move (onto "three"). The left rein keeps the head cocked, the right rein suggests the direction in this early practice. Make sure you stay on your line until you ask the horse to step off of it. When you first begin, release the instant you feel the horse shift or lift his body as if to step to the right. You'll release more on a "relaxation" (or "acquiescence") then any actual sidestepping movement. Build on that, holding till the horse actually takes a step. Repeat till learned.

So, in a nutshell: Bend the head to the left and bring the chin toward the chest. Keep that bend as you take the right rein outward, stare at the spot on the right shoulder, use the right rein to move the spot to the right.

When you can reliably cause the horse to move to the right primarily by using pressure on the outside (your right) rein, begin asking for the horse to move to the right using the LEFT rein. You are transitioning from making your request with a direct rein to an indirect rein. Walk your line and ask the neck to bend to the left slightly then use pressure on the left rein to cause the right shoulder to move to the right. If necessary, use the right rein to prevent the head from "overbending" to the left—and only use it to tell direction if the horse fails to move off the pressure supplied by the left rein.

Here are three traps you should avoid:

If you're walking your line and expect to sidestep to the right, but instead the horse simply turns to the left, lighten up a tad on that left rein—but otherwise keep your hold until the horse accidentally steps correctly (that is, sidesteps to his "new" right). Don't try to steer back onto your line because the extra instruction is confusing. Don't let go even if you're nearing a fence—otherwise you'll teach the horse to find fences. Keep your hold, keep him moving, he'll figure it out.

If you keep losing your bend to the left because your horse is resisting too much through his neck, then you've pushed for too much, too fast. You need to fall back and spend more time softening the neck and getting that chin near the chest. (Do a lot more of those previously-described serpentines.)

That slight bend in the horse's neck is a must. We're teaching the horse to move its shoulder to the right with the left rein and vice versa. If you lose the bend, the horse will most likely simply follow whichever rein applies more pressure—and that's certainly not what we want. This is amazingly common and what you will probably do yourself when you first start. Have patience. If you keep moving and keep your horse's neck rounded, and his chin softly lowered toward the point of his shoulder, you'll eventually step, even if by accident, correctly with those feet. The more relaxed the horse is, the more his chin stays there about five inches from the point of his shoulder, the more likely this will be to happen—keep that one thought running through your head and keep coming back to it if you're having trouble.

A related slip-up is "over-bending" the neck. We're only looking to offset your horse's head by a couple of inches. If the head is way over by your knee you'll get a mess, not a sidestep. This part is critical, underscore the following in your brain: Your horse's head must be only slightly pitched (by a few inches at most) one direction or the other and it must remain there throughout the sidestepping movement. Too much bend and he can't move correctly, no bend and he'll likely turn, following the pull of your rein. Think of it this way: If your horse were made of glass, you'd only want enough bend to break the glass.

If the horse over-bends his neck on his own, you've got several ways to deal with it: 1) Pull it back into position with your "outside rein." (Your "inside" rein is the rein you pick up first; the "outside" rein is the secondary, "helper" rein.) 2) Move your inside rein forward along his neck and literally push it back (which is easier said than done); 3) Ask his hips to move over to re-align his rear (but then right away again ask for your sideways movement; refer to the chapter "Hips, Get Behind the Shoulders"); or 4) Ignore it and let the horse fumble long enough to find the correct step, figuring out for himself how to best position his body (and get you out of his mouth). It's your choice.

You must not let your horse stop through this exercise. Remember dancers Fred and Ginger—and use your legs to bump and keep moving. (At this stage, the legs say "move" but not which direction. Do not use your leg to say "move right.") Even if you move in the wrong direction, at least you're moving. As John Lyons says "First get the foot to move, then get it to move consistently, then get it to move consistently onto the proper spot." Keep the dancer analogy running through your brain, be patient, and really work (really experiment) to find what you have to do (the angles, amounts of pressure, etcetera) to keep your horse moving and eventually "crabbing" smoothly to the right or left. This isn't a wrestling match. Think. Deflect the energy directly right or left, as if a puck on ice.

If your horse wants to stop and back up (also very common), keep your pressure—but dial it back a scosche and try changing your posture. Really think "forward" (doing so will tilt your pelvis, sending a signal to the horse). If that doesn't work, keep your pressure, but take one hand toward the opposite shoulder, asking the hip to disengage. (If you're using your right rein, you'd move it out away from the horse, then back in a nice, round arc toward your left shoulder until the hip steps once to the left.) Disengaging says to the horse "Thanks for moving and all—but I need a different direction or body part." It keeps you fluid and also moves the back feet naturally a step toward the front feet and causes the horse to "lighten up" a bit throughout its entire body. It makes moving the shoulders an easier proposition. You won't be on your shadow line anymore after disengaging, but you can either drop your reins and return to "Step One" or imagine a new line directly in front of your new position.

And finally, PART E: Walk forward, use your right rein to disengage the hips (to the left) and, one beat before the horse stops his hip movement, bring that same rein WAAAY out to the right (away from the horse's mane by a good solid foot) and direct-rein the horse's front feet to the side (to the right). Be patient, wait for the horse to find the step—but do goose him quickly with both legs if you feel a decided loss of impulsion here at this moment. Really focus and experiment to discover the pressure and timing it takes to cause that front foot to step sideways, (and don't pull so much as "guide"). Note that this is usually fairly easy if you get your timing correct and do not allow the horse to stall out: It is critical that you adapt your timing to redirect the horse's momentum from moving his hips to moving his shoulders. If he stops his hips and only then do you swing out that rein, the horse will plant itself. You're just re-channeling energy, so should he stall out altogether, you're finished for better or worse. Get movement, try again: Hips to their left, front feet to their right. This final exercise is terrific for solidifying your timing and ability to "direct-rein" those front feet.

The Reverse Arc Circle

We'll quickly teach the "reverse arc circle" as an example of how to get more advanced shoulder movement using "clock work." "Reverse Arc Circle" is a fancy way of saying "your horse looks off to one side, but pivots on his back foot going the other way," (he looks left, spins right). It's a first step to teaching the reining spin or neck reining.

Prerequisite: A solid knowledge of "The Clockwork Exercise" as previously described.

Do this: Use your left rein to bring your horse's head slightly to the left. Keep the neck slightly bent then as you ask the horse to step its right front foot back and over onto four o'clock. Afterward, release and walk forward. Repeat until this is consistent then ask for two steps onto four o'clock. Then three steps, etcetera. The goal, obviously, is to "step on four" repetitively, pivoting all the way around. I would suggest that when you can get a quarter circle consistently, that you walk straight out ten feet or so, dropping your reins momentarily, then repeat the quarter turn. Walk forward, turn, walk forward, turn. Repeat this pattern and you'll be walking a box pattern. It'll keep you objective and your horse can have time to correctly anticipate your cues and really learn the steps. Practice this box until your horse is proficient at the steps before asking for more (of a circle). (And of course you'll want to become proficient going both to the left and right. Eight o'clock would be the reverse of four in this example.)

To continue on and teach neck reining or a reining spin, you'd begin as described, using the left rein to move right, for instance. You'd then gradually begin applying follow-up pressure with the right rein, asking the horse to look in the direction he's turning, weaning the horse off the left rein as your primary cue. (Becoming proficient at "spinning" requires follow-up exercises—but now you have the tools to teach the fundamentals.)

Tip: Asking your horse to tip his head out of a large circle as he walks (and later when he trots or lopes) is a great way to improve his balance and abilities in general. Try walking, then trotting large, lazy circles with the head tipped out (again, only a few inches, not "at your boot") then challenge yourself to do the same through a figure eight pattern. Try reversing his head in the center point and try every combination (of head carriage vs. direction traveled) you can think of. Keep pushing and you'll be amazed how much lighter your horse gets in the bridle as his balance, muscling, and confidence improves. Pay particular attention to keeping your horse's body upright throughout, (for help there, refer to the following chapter "How to Fix Leaning Shoulders"). Caveat: You must, must, must, take this slowly and only challenge your horse further when he's had time to understand your requests, build the necessary strength and develop his balance. Remember, it requires extra muscle from your horse to keep the both of you raised and level throughout your turns. Give yourself and your horse plenty of time, (as in weeks and months) and back off if you think you may be pushing too hard as evidenced by stalemated improvement or an unusually resistant horse.

How to Fix Leaning Shoulders

If your horse leans over or "drops a shoulder" in a turn, here's how to fix it.

Does your horse tip through its turns? Maybe you've decided you need a "better-fitting" saddle because the one you've got just seems to keep slipping off to the side? (Darned if you don't have to keep readjusting, pumping one stirrup or the other back to center every five minutes, all-the-while thinking "Can my balance really be this bad?") In either case, newsflash: Your horse is "dropping his shoulder." And get this: Not only is the fix easier than you think, it takes effect quicker than you'd expect. Frankly, I wish I'd known this (soon-to-follow) trick twenty years ago—it woulda saved me (and my poor horse) tons of aggravation.

You've probably felt this many times: You turn to the left or right and your thigh and seat tilt downward, leaving your gluteus buttocks sliding off like a pair of fried eggs on a greasy skillet. The fact is, your horse has never been trained to keep upright through his turns. He's simply turning as nature instructs—and Nature doesn't care if you slip off. If you wanna see what properly-trained horses do, take a look at a western reining competition sometime. Reining is a spin to the left one second, a rollback and rundown to a sliding stop the next. Watch specifically for the part of the pattern where the rider is riding his "fast circle" and keep an eye on the horse's overall body positioning, how he keeps both shoulders raised and wholly perpendicular to the ground. You'll see that these well-schooled horses stay very upright as they move—whether they're going fast or slow. Through many miles of wet saddle blankets they've learned that "not leaning" is the only position that allows them to quickly juke from one rider request to the next. They've discovered—on their own, mind you—that leaning makes their lives more difficult while remaining primed for the next movement makes life easier. Here's a demonstration as to the how and why....

Stand up, spread your feet about four feet from each other (or a tad less, depending on your height) and walk one foot around the other. In other words, do the move Curly (of the Stooges fame) used to do. Keep one foot planted in place and pivot by walking the other leg around in a circle like a giant architect's compass. Next, move your legs back together into a natural standing position. Try the same maneuver. Which was easier? Walking unbalanced and spread out—or moving whilst upright? Why, staying upright, of course. If you were a horse and you found yourself asked to do this move frequently, which would you choose? And if you knew that your rider would release his pressure (that is, drop the rein and hence bit pressure) as soon as you completed this move, how long would it take you to begin staying upright all the time?

The fix then, for a horse that leans through his maneuvers, is to ask him to make a move similar to what you just did yourself—and it's the very thing you practiced back in the "Hip Control, Part II" chapter. You'll ask him to "disengage his hindquarters" each time you feel him leaning. If you're loping a "large fast circle," for instance and you feel your horse drop a shoulder, all you need to do is simply slow down and ask the horse to pivot his rear over his front inside shoulder, then immediately go back to your "large fast circle."

They can only disengage smoothly and fluidly when they keep themselves "raised," so you merely need to be insistent, holding your rein pressure steady till he disengages, being quick to release your hold when he does. He'll quickly learn that the quickest way to find relief of your rein pressure is to move correctly—and he'll soon begin keeping himself at the ready. It's more his sense of self-preservation at work than any great love for the task at hand—but why look a gift horse in the mouth?

Here's the one thing you really, really need to understand: The very fact that your horse is leaning will cause him to do his disengagements like garbage at first (remember how hard it was for you?) and you should expect this. He has to be upright (and energized) to pivot correctly, so if he's leaning, he'll most likely drift about or freeze up rather than "lock down" that front foot. Be insistent and keep at it with each occasion until he stops that front foot and pivots with his rear. The moment he does, release—because there, even for a moment he stood upright—and that's what we're rewarding. He'll learn that "spread out" doesn't work, standing upright does.

Which direction to disengage? The direction in which you disengage (that is, which rein you use and which direction his butt moves) isn't all that important despite the direction you might be moving when he leans. But, practically speaking, if you're loping (because this works great for horses that lean over through their faster gaits, too) you'll probably want to use that inside rein (the right rein in a run to the right) simply because your horse is already "curved" in that direction. However... what I've found is that mixing it up is the best route simply because of the horse's habit to begin anticipating. (And dealing with the negative effects of their anticipations is exactly what we're working to remedy here.) They begin to see the corrections coming and can get sort of lazy on you. I deal with this simply by disengaging in random directions when I feel my horse tip. We may be trotting to the right and disengaging with that right rein this minute, disengaging the opposite direction the next. Keep 'em guessing and you'll force them to be prepared for whatever you throw at them. (And that there is the whole point.) Don't overthink it and have fun.

Safety note: Use common sense here and don't go whipping your horse's head around like some crazed bull dogger when moving at higher speed. If the little voice in your head says "Seabiscuit might become unbalanced and trip over himself," then ease up on your pressure, try a different more forgiving angle with your hands, or drop to a slower speed or gait before making your requests. I don't, for instance, expect my horse to disengage "while cantering." I mean, duh, if you're loping and he leans, you'll always need to first break down quickly to a walk or trot and get your disengagement there before resuming your lope. Never ever override that common-sensical little voice.

When you do your disengagements, it is critical that you always walk (or trot or lope) out of the disengagement before fully releasing your pressure—AND for there to be zero hesitation in the interim. Your very success is directly tied to this fact. Failing to move forward at the end of the exercise will cause the horse to lower (that is, to "drop" or "relax") the very body parts we're trying to keep raised as he starts to anticipate a premature end to the maneuver. We want him to be thinking "What's next?" not "Stop and hang out." Also note that you'll see quicker results if you swap sides often, practicing the routine "going the other way."

Serpentine: Indirect to Direct

Here's an additional exercise that'll teach your horse to stay "upright" through his travels and put an end to "corner cutting."

Prerequisite: The ability to independently move your horse's shoulders left or right using both direct and indirect reins.

In a typical, simple, serpentine exercise, you might turn the horse using a direct rein (that is, to turn left, you placed pressure on the left rein), traveled forward a beat or two, then direct-reined the opposite direction. But now try the following: At a trot, use an indirect rein to bring your horse's shoulders over a step, pause a beat, then change your thoughts (and the angle or pressure on the same rein) to "direct-rein" the horse into a graceful turn in the opposite direction—that is, a single (right) rein asks for the shoulders to move left, then for the horse to turn right or vice versa.

Example: Move off and pick up the left rein and ask the shoulders to step to the right. Lessen the pressure on the rein when you believe the horse is about to step to the right to signal "correct"—but one beat later use that same rein to ask the horse to step to the left. You want that secondary "step to the left" to be forward, in a smooth arc, not abrupt or side-stepping. The hips must travel squarely behind the shoulders. You move somewhat sideways in the first half but curve out in a fluid and forward turn during the second.

(The pause in between movements is critical. It rewards the horse and clearly defines the beginning and end of each request. Should you find your horse becoming confused, ask yourself if you're not skipping that brief and necessary pause.)

Tip: Don't over-think the direction at which you should hold the rein at any point. The horse doesn't really care from which direction the pressure comes from—the horse only wants you out of his mouth. What your horse will react to are the small changes you unconsciously make in your body when you move your focus. "When you think different, you carry yourself differently." Changing your focal point from "turn left" to "turn right" will cause you to reflexively change the tilt of your pelvis, the weight carried in one stirrup or the other, the pressure and direction you place on the reins, etcetera. Don't think "I hold the rein 'this way' to 'make' the shoulders move," think "I hold the rein until the horse 'understands' my request, 'move your shoulders.'"

We're asking for two entirely different movements with rein cues that are very similar. Given that, if the horse misses a cue, it's probably not a matter of adding "motivation," so much as figuring out another way to ask: If your horse has difficulty turning correctly off a direct rein (if it keeps going straight ahead or leaks out from the turn), then use that same rein to ask the hips to step across, forcing a change of direction. If you're asking for the shoulders to step across with an indirect rein and the horse simply leans on the rein or turns incorrectly, then maintain your hold on the outside rein in order to keep the neck bent and the head looking away from the direction of travel, but raise your second rein and concentrate on asking the horse to step across using direct-rein pressure. Do exactly what you would have done in the Clockwork Exercise to cause the horse to step sideways; your left rein says "nine," your right rein says "three" and vice versa. Use both reins together until the horse gets the idea and when the shoulders begin to move, drop the second "direct" rein you picked up; a quick moment later you would drop the "indirect" rein. This is a big part of why we practiced the Clockwork material – so that we'd have two ways to say the same thing if it became necessary.

Common pitfall: With this exercise you will necessarily "wander all over the place." Do not try to direct your horse beyond what is prescribed. If you find yourself drifting toward the gate, then so be it; practice at the gate. If you find yourself carried near a buddy horse, fine, practice near that buddy horse. The horse will soon learn that dodges like this do him little good. Stay proactive and objective by concentrating intensely on the "dance pattern" as outlined and you win. Lose your focus and muck about—and your time spent training is lost.

Speed Control
Basic Speed Control

Presently, your horse knows just two speeds: "Slow" going away from the barn and "fast" going toward it. Here we teach it to slow down and speed up when lightly cued—but also to travel consistently at a wide range of speeds.

Prerequisite: The ability to move your horse's hips and shoulders left and right. Refer to the chapters "Hip Control, Part II" and "Shoulder Control."

When you first put a saddle on your horse, the horse didn't know if it was a forever thing and it probably bucked. The idea is similar here. When you ask for a particular speed, the horse doesn't know that he'll be allowed to stop at that gate over there so he might very well speed up or slow down to register his discontent. The work described here teaches the horse that he can do what is expected. It teaches your horse to travel at a constant rate and an ever-broadening range of speeds.

In a safe environment, mount up and cue for a trot. Sit as you would normally and after a few beats, use both reins to ask the horse to slow down. Search out the slowest speed your horse will travel for at least ten feet with zero pressure on the reins. We're not looking for "How slow can the horse go for two seconds when I pull back with the reins?" We're looking for "What's the slowest this horse will go without me constantly pulling on its mouth?" Find the slowest speed you can get consistently for ten or so feet with no pressure on the reins and ask yourself how many miles an hour you were traveling. Lock that speed and feeling into memory.

Next, lean forward just a hair, move your hands (and thus the reins) forward, kiss, cluck like a chicken, do what you do to ask your horse to move faster. Give your cue or cues once, bump with your legs if necessary, then back off. Find the fastest speed you can get—for ten or more feet—with a single request. If it breaks into a lope, ease it back down to a trot. Assign a number to your highest rate of travel and remember it.

In that test, your horse might very well go from "trotting" to "not trotting." There may not be much of a difference between "fast" and "slow." That's okay, it just means your horse hasn't learned a speed control cue; teaching this is the very point of this exercise.

Let's say the slow speed you clock is six, the faster speed eleven. (The numbers are just a guess made by you, an approximation to serve as a yardstick.) At the trot, your horse is capable of traveling in that narrow collection of speeds, 6 to 11, today. You can improve things by practicing many changes of speed within that range (ONLY WITHIN THAT RANGE) and by consciously asking your horse to speed up or slow down BEFORE IT DOES SO ON ITS OWN. Practice what follows first at a trot, later at a lope. Note that any practice done in one gait will have a positive impact on the other gaits as your horse learns to wait for your cues to speed up and slow down. Also note that simply practicing lots of speed transitions within the boundaries your horse first gives you (6 to 11 in this example) will have the effect of expanding those very boundaries. (So, you might be able to travel between 6 and 11 today—but practicing this exercise might get you 4 to 14 next month.)

Regardless of whether your horse moves too fast or too slow (or whether you simply want to expand the range of speeds available), you'll improve things in the same way. The answer isn't to pull on the reins constantly to slow down nor is it a matter of incessant kicking to stay in a particular speed. Instead, the answer lies in teaching all horses two cues, one to speed up, one to slow down. If your horse goes too fast, he's plainly never learned a cue to slow down. But he doesn't know the cue to move faster either, as evidenced by the fact that he speeds up on his own. He doesn't wait for a cue; he doesn't even know one exists. We want this horse to learn two things: 1) Respect our cue to slow down and 2) Wait for our cue to speed up. The same can be said, in reverse, for the horse that won't reliably accelerate. He ignores our cue to speed up and he doesn't wait for our cue to slow down.

Here's what you do: Cue your horse to trot quickly on a forty foot circle to the left. Travel no more than ten to twenty feet before asking the horse to slow down, using BOTH reins. Don't insist on a dramatic change in speeds. You just want "slower," anything within the lower range of speeds your horse gave you in your test. Throughout this exercise, you can keep both reins in your hands, using them to cue your horse to slow but also to direct-rein it back onto your circle when and if you drift away. Be sure to keep slack in those reins when not actively using them.

Trot 10 to 20 feet at that slower speed, with no rein pressure, before asking the horse to speed up, then travel 10 to 20 feet at that quicker speed and slow down. With each of your speed transitions, you are looking for a "noticeable change of leg speed." It's not a maybe, it's a definitely. It's a definite, noticeable change of leg speed. Repeat this sequence for a solid twenty minutes. In doing so, it is very important that you cue for your speed transitions before the horse slows down or speeds up on its own. If it slows without a cue from you after trotting 18 feet, next time ask it to change at 17. In time, your horse will learn to wait for your cues, traveling at the speed you choose for the distance you choose.

Don't travel more than 20 feet without cuing for a change of speed because that cue is exactly what your horse needs to learn. The more changes in speed, the more you get to practice the cue. Pick any faster or slower speed from within the range given to you in the test above, not necessarily the slowest or fastest.

If your horse does not slow on light pressure, do not pull harder on the reins to force the issue. Motivate it to do so by moving the shoulders left then right, left then right. If moving the shoulders has no effect, turn the horse's hips aside as you've practiced. The more you turn the hips, the more the horse will slow. Given this, you might find yourself heading back the other direction on your circle—and that's fine—but do stay on your circle and remember to always drop your rein pressure as soon as possible. (Refer to the chapters "Slow Down, Part I" and "Slow Down, Part II" for further guidance.) When moving either the shoulders or hips, use primarily one rein as you've learned previously, then immediately return to using both reins to guide your horse and to cue it initially to slow down.

You must only ask for a speed from within the range you were given in the test. If turning the horse's shoulders or hips gets a slower trot than you got back in your test and the horse will travel this way for ten or more feet without rein pressure—great—but don't make it happen by nagging with those reins. Don't try to "force it" to go slower. New speeds will come on their own when you simply practice the material as written. This is important to understand because, while you might be able to pull on the horse or move his hips to and fro to cause it to slow down, if it won't travel at that speed for more than a few feet before changing on its own, then you don't get to practice your cue—and so it does you no good. There's also this: Pulling the horse down into an unfamiliar or unnaturally slow speed will cause it to frequently break to a walk, then you'll have to ask it to trot over and over, muddying the training waters, confusing your horse.

To recap, this is all you will do: Trot a large circle and use both reins to slow the horse. Trot slowly for 10-20 feet then cue the horse to speed up. Trot another 10-20 feet quickly and slow down again. Quick, slow, quick, slow. 10 feet one moment, 5 or 10 or 15 the next. Mix and match speeds and distances. Over and over and over.

I need you to remember the next sentence; write it on a scrap of paper and tape it to the fridge next to the recipe for thumbprint cookies: Your CUE to slow is always light rein pressure; your MOTIVATOR to slow is always a movement of the shoulders or hips. Here, rein pressure is a cue, so you only ask with light to moderate pressure and consciously work to use less and less. Asking the shoulders or hips to move, that's motivation; use them to reinforce your rein cue. Don't pull the horse to go slower because that's confusing your "cue" with your "motivator." Remember, you're doing this work because your horse has been ignoring your cue to slow down, so be very careful not to burn it out here.

Take note:

- When you ask for increased speed, you must keep squeezing or bumping your horse with the same tempo and force until the horse speeds up. If you tire and stop kicking, you will succeed only in teaching the horse that kicking means "don't speed up" or even "plant yourself right here." This means that you must keep kicking at the same intensity for as long as it takes to speed your horse up—be that half a minute, half an hour, or half a day. You don't want to start off with a big kick if you can't keep it up for as long as it takes.

- Don't badger your horse to "stay in a speed." If you think the horse is about to slow down on his own, resist the urge to egg him on faster with a kick or squeeze. That makes sense to you ("He's about to slow down; I'll prevent that")—but the horse figures he got kicked for no good reason. Your kisses, clucks, squeezes and kicks (your "move faster" cues and motivators) will burn out and you'll soon find yourself kicking constantly just to briefly travel at a chosen speed. Instead, move the horse up to a higher speed when you feel him begin to slow. (That is, if he slows to "four miles an hour," forget "four" and move him to "five.") Travel a few beats at the faster rate, then turn and pick up an altogether different speed.

Throughout your practice, be conscious of the pressure you keep on the rein and the timing of your releases. Don't "just" work on speed control—kill two birds with one stone by trying to soften your horse's response through the reins every time you pick them up. Always hold your pressure until you feel a softening through the reins. By the same token, watch your horse's frame and how it carries itself. Don't allow it to throw its head in the air when you cue it to speed up. As described in the chapter "Softening," you want the horse to carry itself smoothly through its transitions. Should it start to throw its head up and out, rushing forward all splayed out, hold your rein pressure until you feel a relaxation and work to keep that head into proper position. Don't allow earlier training to suffer—always be working for improvement.

Remember that adding speed adds emotion, and that probably means increased stiffness throughout his body. Be on the lookout for this and employ a zero tolerance policy toward any sort of resistance in the form of bracing, stiff muscles, lurching, etcetera. If your horse becomes stiff as you increase speed, cancel your plans to work on speed control for the moment and instead work on softening. (Do serpentines: Pick up a single rein as he turns, hold the rein till his neck relaxes or drops, walk forward, repeat the other way—again and again with an eye toward calming your horse. Alternatively, you can practice your disengagements. Repeatedly turning the back end is a quick route to softening the front end.)

Don't forget that your horse doesn't really know something, some bit of training, if it doesn't do it every time you ask, in all situations. This is an especially good thing to bear in mind when it comes to speed control. It's not good enough that your horse speeds up or slows down in the arena under controlled circumstances, this is control you need to diligently build into your horse so that in high-stress moments, you've got something to call upon. If a dove flies from a tree and your horse bolts—you need the ability to slow it down. If you'd like to catch up to friends on the trail, you need to speed up in a safe and controlled manner. In those moments, you either have control or you do not – and it's too late to do anything about it if you do not. Don't guess; don't leave this to chance. Consciously seek out creative spots or situations to test the control you've acquired. When your horse will travel consistently at a new range of speeds while circling as outlined above, practice this on a straightaway. When proficient there, when you feel the two of you are ready, ask a friend or two or three to take a working trail ride with you. The added distraction of a few buddy horses will lend an extra layer of difficulty and give you more opportunity to install solid control that you can depend on in good times and bad.

Slow Down, Part I: Move the Hip

If you have problems with your horse getting "higher and higher"—or need ways to slow a fast one down—then the following two sections are for you.

The crux of the training in this segment is teaching ourselves to divert a horse's energy to our purposes rather than fighting it. Attempting to bottle up the fractious horse, of course, results in nasty behavior like rearing, bolting and bucking. So, rather than trying to contain it, we vent off some of that steam.

Pick up a trot (or a walk if you feel it necessary) and do the following:

Step 1) Pick up your right rein and find the angle and amount of pressure it takes to move the horse's butt one step to the left BUT KEEP MOVING FORWARD then release the rein and trot on. Relax a beat or two and compose your thoughts, then repeat the sequence for twenty minutes. Do not worry about "where" you're going; do not try to steer.

Step 2) There is no Step Two. How simple is that? You've calmed an agitated horse and it took one brain cell to do it. It's just "pick up the rein, move the hip over, drop the rein." This is idiot proof.

When to use this: This is typically used to slow down a horse that wants to go too fast, instilling basic "slow down" speed control. However, exerting this control over your horse's hips will also go a long way to controlling horses that threaten to rear, bolt or buck, lessening the likelihood of a wreck. When you see a bad situation coming, dissipate the pressure by asking for his hip to move over a step, then relaxing a beat before repeating the movement until you feel he has calmed enough to continue. Employ this anytime you feel your horse's emotions bubbling up to diffuse and avoid altercations.

How this works: When a horse gets excited, he tends to become rigid and move faster. Asking his hips to take a step across upholds your control over a single body part while slowing him with no fuss, no muss. It slows the horse in the same way a boat would be slowed (from moving forward) if you were to pick up the rear end and move it slightly to the right. For a moment all that power stops driving forward and just dissipates.

Second, by simply picking up the rein till he takes a step over and releasing, your horse never feels trapped. He doesn't stop moving forward and he learns to deal with pressure. (No need to fight, you're not cutting off his flight.)

It has the bonus, cumulative effect of causing your horse to relax his neck and drop his high head. It accomplishes this because the horse learns that when you pick up the reins, you're not looking for a wrestling match—you just want him to move his hips. You'll find that practicing this will soften even the toughest-mouthed horse.

Here are three things to remember:

1) Don't allow the horse to stop moving—and keep the tempo. The whole point is to get the horse to give while he's moving.

2) Make sure that you relax the reins in between repetitions. Otherwise the horse thinks it's a twenty minute exercise. More importantly, he won't be getting a break from your pressure so he won't calm down. (This is very, very important.)

3) If you lose your concentration and meander around (and don't do this for 20+ minutes) your results will suffer.

If your horse becomes agitated when you try to turn his hips, fall back in your training. Re-start from a point where both of you were working well together.

The objective here is to further teach the horse to "give to pressure." (To not pull away from the bit, but rather to relax his muscles and to bend fluidly, evenly.) So if you just can't get the horse to move that hip over, or you don't feel safe "forcing the issue," or if you feel like you're trying to bend a two thousand pound rock, then make it simpler for both of you: Walk off and pick up a single rein, applying the lightest of pressure. Wait till he softens his neck muscles or drops his head (even the slightest little bit) as he takes a step in the same direction. Then let go, praise, repeat. What do you do if you can't get even that? (Say, the horse backs, stops, etcetera.) Again, make it simpler: Get that forward motion, pick up a rein, wait till the head softens or drops without asking for any sort of turn. When you get that, try "softening on the turn" before again asking for the hips to move.

Slow Down, Part II: Wherein We Train the Brain

When you want to teach your horse to slow down, a simple key is to find a moment when traveling on a loose rein and build on it.

If you are constantly tugging on the reins to get your horse to slow down, then what you're really doing is teaching it two things: 1) Pressure from your legs is not the cue to speed up and 2) A loose rein is the cue to speed up.

Huh? How can that be?

It's simple. If you start nagging with the reins when the horse starts moving too fast, look at what's happening from your horse's perspective: "When I'm slowing down, she pulls on my mouth. Aha! If I want a release, I gotta speed up." And, if you constantly bump with your legs, getting little to no change from your horse as you do so, you're teaching it that leg bumps mean nothing. Couple that thought with your horse's "fight or flight" instinct ("I'm gonna run or buck if I can't get away")—and you've built a rocket to ride.

Your horse will never travel on a loose rein if you never let go of the reins. You must proactively and consciously ease up on those reins and create your own "teachable moments." Even if you feel that your horse is constantly pulling and tugging on the reins like a struggling pack of Alaskan huskies, look for those brief instances when your horse isn't pulling "as hard" on you and build on that. If necessary, fabricate those moments by putting the horse to work, asking for more and more until slowing down, (aka "slacking off") however briefly, is a natural reaction.

When you're on the trail and your horse begins moving his feet too fast or dances about, ask him to do some small task that he's already good at. Do some simple exercise like a serpentine (as detailed in "Classic Serpentine") or "trot twenty feet, turn, trot twenty feet, turn," or a simple movement like "move your shoulder to the right one step" (then pause and repeat, pause and repeat). Put him to work, doing something easy, objective and repetitious for several minutes, feeling all the while for a brief moment when you release the rein AND YOU CAN FEEL THE HORSE WANTING TO SLOW for any reason.

If time passes and the horse continues to rush, then give him exponentially more to do, make things more complicated. Maybe "move your hips to the right" becomes "move your hips to the right, then drop your head, then soften your neck, then move your shoulder, then..." etcetera. Don't up your own intensity level, just put more on his plate. Pile enough on and you'll find your moment.

You may have a horse that wants to take off at a dead run if you give him back any amount of rein. If that's the case, then try your level best to ride with the least amount of pressure you can and each time the horse begins to speed up, take a single rein and turn his tail "the way you don't want to go." Example: Your horse speeds up so you take the left rein and apply the pressure it takes to get the left shoulder to stop and the hip to move several steps to the right. Ride forward and repeat, looking for some brief hesitation signaling that your horse wants to slow up. (Disengaging those back legs drains power as we've learned and it does so without igniting a fight.)

In all cases, in that fraction of time when you feel him slow, you have two options:

1) Ride slower, move slower, see how long the "moment" lasts—and QUIT the extra exercise. Go back to your quiet trail ride. The horse thinks "Funny, I slowed down and suddenly I didn't have to work so hard." When the horse speeds up again (perhaps one second later, maybe two minutes later) then go back to the exercise (rather intensely) and wait for him to signal that he'd like to move slowly. Then you quit again. The horse comes to associate hard work with shenanigans and will start to think twice before acting up.

Or, try:

2) Ride slower, move slower, see how long the "moment" lasts—and CONTINUE the exercise. Beyond teaching your horse to calm down, this second option will go further toward training it in other aspects: He'll turn to the right sharper, stay softer, etcetera. Plus, while sharpening his performance, you will have captured his attention and made it easier to get it the next time.

Both options work. Experiment to see which is right for you, when and where. See what produces results and adapt.

Be careful to stay focused and feel for the horse softening—sometimes we start pulling so hard we don't realize that the horse couldn't relax even if he wanted to.

By practicing this material, (and by "thinking differently" as outlined) you will teach your horse to rate his speed and you will do so safely, without a fight. Along the way you will also improve its overall performance, creating a horse that is safer to ride, picks up his leads more reliably, trots more comfortably, moves more smoothly and is a pleasure to ride.

The key is this: You've got to look for every opportunity to relax those reins. Quit pulling. Horses aren't nags, neither should you be.

Balky Horses: Comatose One Minute, Hot to Trot the Next

Here's what to do when your horse moves slower and slower on the way out of the barn—but faster and faster when headed toward it. Plus: The horse that won't move.

Note: If your horse is altogether ignoring your leg cue to speed up, review the earlier chapter "Speed Control" and the opening chapter, "Legs Mean Move."

Forcing a horse to speed up when headed in a direction he does not want to go is begging for a wreck. And when this same horse wants to race the others back home and you take a death grip on the reins in an effort to simply slow down, there you are again, another clash on your hands. You've got one horse and two problems, a horse that won't speed up and a horse that won't slow down. Address both with this exercise, an exercise that's perfect for the horse that's just spoiling for a fight.

If you're headed out to the trail (heading away from the barn) and your horse begins to walk increasingly slower—most likely because he's thinking about heading home to his stall with or without you—and you think there's a good chance he's about to freeze up completely... then try the following: Turn 90 degrees back toward the barn. As you do, you'll feel him speed up, because he thinks he's going home. (If 90 degrees doesn't speed him up, try 100, 110, etcetera, but only as much as it takes for him to speed up and travel more openly on his own.) You'll next take a single rein and direct him back a few degrees toward the direction you'd like to go. Quit thinking about either going away from the barn or to the barn and start moving back and forth like a snake at right angles to the trail, using his natural forward impulsion (each time he's turned toward the barn) to propel and energize your movement. Moving freely down the trail is a goal, moving smoothly is the immediate task at hand. Remember, and this is important, get off his mouth, quit kicking and RELAX anytime he improves by even one half of one percent.

Your job is to get the horse moving smoothly—in any direction—in a controlled manner: When he moves fluidly, turn him a degree or two away from the barn. When he slows and you need to add energy to the equation, capitalize on his eagerness to get home by turning him a degree or two back toward the barn. In time, his speed will even out, so basically, you've gotta be more stubborn than the horse. It doesn't take them long to recognize an inexperienced rider, right? Well, it doesn't take the savvy horse long to realize when you've got his number either.

Make your corrections when you're moving at a 90 degree angle relative to the trail. Use that time to teach. He'll be far more likely to react positively to you when not directed 180 degrees away from where he'd really rather be. Concentrate on fluid motion and kick or correct only when you feel a slower "noticeable change of leg speed." Walk (or trot) a slalom pattern, like a skier and try to put life, electricity and rhythm into your travel.

Try this work at a trot if you feel safe doing so. Walking through this work runs the risk of a "bog down," with the two of you moving slower and slower. Don't ever forget: The energy you put into your ride is the energy you'll get out of your ride. Also, remember that once you begin kicking, you're locked into kicking at that strength at that same pace from now until something hot freezes over or he moves. So think before you kick and pick your battles carefully.

If you're thinking "But my rider friends are moving away and it's only my horse that wants to stop. Dick, Jane and Sally won't wait for me to train." Uh, sorry—get more understanding friends or stay in the arena till you get this licked. You're putting yourself in a dangerous situation if you force the horse through this (forcing it ahead, down the trail) and it's going to get worse if you ignore it. Take the time to deal with this correctly and your insurance agent will thank me.

Frozen in place: What do we do with the horse that locks up and won't budge? If your horse locks up, refusing to cross an obstacle (such as a creek), look to the upcoming chapter, "Crossing Creeks and Scary Stuff". If your horse has locked up for no discernible reason (other than simply "I'm not gonna move and you can't make me"), you'll do exactly what we learned to do with the young horse first learning leg and rein cues (back in the chapter called "Legs Mean Move"): You pick up the rein and pull the horse's head off to one side by a few inches, let's say four. Let your rein go completely—and when the horse takes its head back forward, pull it back to the side. Don't pull the horse's head into place and hold it there—the horse will feel trapped. Get it into place and drop your rein. It may take several repetitions before the horse will simply leave his head askew, just keep putting it back into place, four or so inches to the side.

Don't start by wrenching his head to your knee—because where would you go from there if you need to send a more pointed message? (Besides, such a sharp angle makes it exceedingly difficult for him to move so you'd be creating a bigger obstacle.)

We want the back legs to step over. (Pick up the left rein, the hip should move to the right.) Wait long enough and what you'll feel is the horse shifting his weight in order to take a step, moving the hips-into alignment with this head and neck. (If he moves a front leg first, just hold until the back leg moves.) The millisecond you feel the horse shift his weight to move that rear end, let go of the reins, thrust those hips forward (yours) and try to ride out of your predicament. Really believe you're gonna go someplace. Of course, you may go absolutely nowhere—but a positive attitude will be read by your horse. It makes no difference if he moves but a quarter of an inch or even leans forward—it only matters that you reward the correct thought. If he moves even the slightest, drop your reins, pet him and take a two second break.

Do the same thing again. And again. Collect enough of these hip movements, string them together closely, and you'll soon find yourself moving forward. More often than not, you only have to repeat this half a dozen times or so and they'll just walk off as you ask, having learned that freezing up gets them nowhere (literally). You got him moving—and you did it without a fight. Then, if he's moving but drags when pointed away from home, refer back to the beginning of this chapter.

And finally, what do you do if the horse seems content to just move his hips to and fro with no reasonable end in sight? Try getting off the horse and working it from the ground as instructed in the "Hip Control" chapter.

Spend time moving the horse's shoulders, disengaging his back legs, asking him to move forward (especially forward) and backward. Teach him that one way or the other, he's going to move. Standing on the ground keeps you a bit safer when dealing with such a horse and you'll have the opportunity to get him thinking about your requests and to forget his tantrum. When you get back home, spend LOTS of time practicing the "Speed Control" exercises. Get your horse in the habit of saying "yes" to your requests, quashing future temper tantrums before they start. (For additional insight, look ahead to the chapter "Training Magic: Release on the Thought.")

Crossing Creeks and Scary Stuff

Forcing your horse across obstacles without proper training is inviting trouble. Here's how to properly prepare your horse to walk across scary objects like tarps and water and to avoid fights. It's also great pre-training for teaching your horse to load into a trailer.

Prerequisite: Mastery of the material covered in the chapter "Teach Your Horse to Lower Its Head While Standing"

Katrina R. in Cripple Creek, CO writes:

My horse acts like he might buck and rear when I ask him to go across our creek. It happens anytime we get near water—puddles are a nightmare. He's gonna kill me if I ever get caught out riding in the rain. I tried for two hours yesterday and never got across the creek outside because I was afraid to push him. What do I do?

Pushing your horse across something frightening, skipping the intermediary training (as I'll outline shortly), is pushing your horse into "fight or flight" mode—which can easily leave you in the dust. You did the right thing by backing off and looking for a training plan.

Begin your training on the ground and get into the saddle to tackle creek crossing only after the horse learns to move forward under a variety of conditions.

First, teach your horse a cue to move forward over flat ground when asked: Stand on the horse's left side and take the lead in your hand. Raise a dressage whip toward his hip and pause. Think "forward." Your horse will stand there. Start tapping on the high point of his rump with even pressure, the idea being that you will release all pressure (including your grip on the lead) the moment the horse so much as leans forward. Just keep tapping, increasing pressure right up to the point of "being really irritating."

Stop tapping the moment you get the horse to move forward and sooner rather than later he'll begin simply stepping forward as you raise your arms. You always want to work with the least amount of motivation possible, so make it a game to see how little pressure it takes to get him moving consistently. It'll take tapping when you first begin, and simply the raising of your arm shortly thereafter.

When your horse will consistently move forward over an even surface, lay out several poles (or boards or PVC pipe. Here in south Texas, we'd use cedar stays). Place them a few feet apart and ask your horse to cross them. Circle back around and practice moving across the poles at a wide variety of speeds UNTIL HE DOES NO'T SMACK HIS FEET as he steps and is relaxed, then practice going the other way.

Next: Clear away the poles and lay out a surface (better yet, "surfaces" plural) that offers a bit more of a test. You might nail together a large square with 2x4s then fill the area with odd footing such as deep gravel, piled hay, or an old garden hose. Just find something that adds challenge. You might simply drop a sheet of plywood into place or maybe an old door. Don't spend a bunch of money; use what you've got on hand. Ask your horse to repeatedly cross this from all directions. Be creative and remember that there is no such thing as too much practice. Note that sometimes – with certain obstacles and certain horses – you'll find it easier to first walk the front half of the horse onto (and then off) the object, then turn about and walk the back half of the horse over the object, before attempting to push the entire horse across. (Be adaptable and think "out of the box" with your training; don't get locked into any specific approach. If one door's locked, try another.)

Next: Place a series of large objects, such as 40-gallon rain-water barrels, in a straight row running parallel to a fence. (The space between the barrels and fence should be just a bit wider than your horse.) Practice your "go forward cue," moving your horse back and forth through the narrow channel. This will challenge the horse to tackle his fear of enclosed spaces – and therefore give you a chance to build in even more control. (When trailer training, be sure to include this common exercise. It offers obvious parallels to loading a horse.) Be sure to practice traveling through the "channel" from both your left and right.

You can, of course, add as many steps into this process as time will allow, but I'd add at least one more; I'd put down a tarp. (Because getting your horse "used to" that crinkly potato-chip bag sound the tarp makes with each step goes a mile toward despooking your horse—you're getting two birds with one stone.) As you lay out the tarp, be sure to anchor the edges and sides down with ties or something heavy. (Tarps have a habit of getting stuck to hooves like Velcro; you don't need the extra hassle right off the bat of having the tarp come flying up around your horse's legs.) Stand off to the side and near the horse's shoulder as you walk alongside; you don't want to get flattened if it spooks. (For extra credit, save up a dozen or so plastic milk cartons of varying sizes and place those under the tarp.)

With all of these intermediary training steps, you want to spent plenty of time walking the horse forward a foot or two, then ask it to back up, forward two or three feet, then back, and so on. Consciously and proactively work to totally eliminate any "stop" between the forward and backward movement. (That is, you don't want a pause of any length whatsoever in that transitioning period between moving ahead and backing up. It's not "Forward. Stop. Back up," it's "forwardbackward.") Your goal is to feel absolutely no "push back" through your grip on the halter; you want zero resistance, even when abruptly changing directions. Keep your dressage whip handy, ready to add motivation should your horse begin to drag through the exercise. Remember: The energy you put in is the energy you get out.

Next, mount up. Walk towards the object (a creek in this case), looking ahead and deliberately choosing a very precise point at which you intend to cross. You'll not cross three feet to the left or sixteen feet to the right; you will cross right there. Lock that location in your mind's eye.

Note from the outset that your objective is to move to, over, and past the object (creek, tarp, bridge, what-have-you) at a consistent, unvarying rate of speed. Through every moment of the training which follows, concentrate and consciously work to keep the horse's feet falling at the same pace before, during, and after your crossing. Granted, the two of you might very well slow to a crawl or freeze up entirely at first – but smooth movement squelches little moments of hesitation in which your horse may get second thoughts. Additionally, when you can move across evenly, with lightness and purpose, you'll objectively know that the lesson is learned.

If your horse is going to inevitably balk at crossing the creek, then some distance away (maybe ten feet, maybe forty) it will become hesitant. One moment you're walking ahead with an even cadence, the next the horse's head is up and it wants to turn back. Make note of the spot where you first feel resistance—and return to this area (actually, just before it) if or when your horse gets overly agitated; it's where you'll reinstall calm and control. Think of it as a neutral corner or the horse's "happy place." Go there to relax the horse, doing some simple exercise like a serpentine, and then re-approach the creek. Doing what it takes to keep things calm helps assure your horse that there's no need to put up a fight, you'll not force it to do something scary.

As you near the water's edge, ask your horse to drop its head near to the ground. You're saying "We're going to cross this thing, get in position to do so." (Refer to the prerequisite chapter "Teach Your Horse to Lower Its Head While Standing.") When you ask for this, be sure to do so far enough away from your crossing point that the horse has plenty of time to ready himself. Don't forget to factor in your speed – a faster rate of travel calls for a greater distance. Note: Dropping your horse's head on command is something you need to be good at before tackling obstacle crossing of any kind because you don't want a wrestling match on your approach; doing so would negate any and all rhythm and fluidity.

If and when your horse freezes up completely, don't push it forward, just let it stand and be calm a moment. Keep its head near the ground, pointed at your "spot." Each and every time it looks away bring it back into position: Down and pointed ahead. (You'll likely have to put your horse's head back as described a hundred times or more because the more they don't want to cross, the more they'll look away for alternative routes.) If it wants to sniff the water or paw, that's fine. Allow it to do so for as long as it likes. These actions simply mean your horse is thinking about crossing but needs time to diagnose the situation. Remember, it's just a shallow creek to you – but it's a life or death decision as far as your horse is concerned.

After a brief pause, bump your horse with your legs IF YOU BELIEVE THERE IS A REASONABLE CHANCE THAT IT'LL MOVE. (If, instead, you feel that kicking will not cause the horse to move or that you might be asking for trouble – or if much time has passed and all you seem to be getting are evasive maneuvers – skip to "Troubleshooting" below.) Understand that your bumping just means "move" so you'll have to accept any movement at all here. This is important: If your horse moves its feet – regardless the direction – stop bumping immediately and allow yourself to be carried. (Caution: If your horse backs up and seems frightened or agitated, see "Troubleshooting," below) If you keep kicking while the horse is frozen solid or moving in the wrong direction, he'll soon figure he might as well just stand there and get kicked (or worse, you might pick a real fight). As you progress and the horse relaxes, he'll be more apt to move forward than the other directions.

You might get one or two steps, you might get just a lean – maybe you'll simply feel the back feet creep forward. Those are all good answers because when you add up enough movement, you've got your crossing – and once your horse learns there's nothing to fear, future crossings get pretty easy. The key here is that you must stay focused like a laser. No matter where the horse takes you or which way you travel, keep your eyes and the horse's nose pointed toward your crossing spot. That's all you think about. You might sail to the side and his hips might be waaaay over here and his nose waaaay over there—but your mind needs to stay locked on that six inches of dirt or tarp or water's edge like a dog with a bone to clearly signal your intent to the horse. "We are going to that spot."

The less familiar you are with the horse you're riding, the less experience you have as a rider or the horse has packing folks around, the more excited the horse seems to be, the less you want to start kicking hard and "forcing" things. The more reticent your horse, the less you should demand. When in doubt, play things cool (see "Troubleshooting," below) because a horse might very well rear up and put you on the ground rather than move through/onto/across something that seems terrifying. He might very well be thinking that you're just too dumb to realize that that there is a horse-eating rock and he'll take matters into his own hands, thanks very much. Use common sense and don't force a rebellion.

When your horse first moves into the creek with a foot or two, he might very well decide to simply jump over the whole thing if it's not too great a distance. Be ready for such a lurch and when you get to the other side, travel a safe distance away, then turn back and repeat this same process, being sure to once again pick out a very small spot to cross. Your horse might jump the creek a number of times, but he'll soon learn that it isn't necessary and he'll just walk across when the mystery dissolves. Practice this until there is zero hesitation from your horse as you cross from both directions. Just doing it a couple times doesn't mean he's learned it—and I'm sure you'd rather not repeat your training tomorrow when your friends are alongside!

TROUBLESHOOTING: If your horse backs away from the obstacle or water's edge and seems frightened or agitated, DO NOT touch the reins as it backs up. Picking up the reins might cause your horse to rear in such a circumstance. Allow yourself to be carried until the horse stops of its own accord. As you move, turn and look back to make sure the two of you are not headed toward something truly dangerous (e.g., a barbed wire fence or drop off). If you see trouble, step off and let the horse go on its own. Otherwise – and what will typically happen – is that your horse will back to a point that it considers a safe distance from "the thing." When you do come to a halt, stand a moment then carefully pick up the reins and practice some simple exercise to regain "calm."

If you find yourself sitting there on your horse, stuck in your training – the horse won't move and you're tired of badgering – don't be afraid to move away briefly to "re-boot" your collective brain. Sometimes simply moving off and trotting a circle or two in a lazy fashion will re-start stalled training. Anytime you "don't know what else to do," just head back to the horse's "happy place" and practice 60 seconds of anything. But don't stand there, don't stop moving – the only place you should be standing is up there at your crossing spot.

If your horse won't take another step forward – and the voice in your head says that kicking won't do any good (or might prove dangerous), then move some fifty feet away from your spot and practice moving forward, then backward, forward, then backward. Work to take out the "stop" there in the middle, just as you did previously on the ground. Get the horse extra-super practiced in the art of saying "yes" to your "go forward" request from the saddle.

If your horse continues to balk and you need a bit more motivation: Practice some exercise – any exercise – just to the left and right of your crossing spot and be intense about it. Not heavy-handed, scary, or aggressive, just intense like a drill sergeant. This is a page out of basic trailer training: Show the horse that the only place he can relax is there on the small patch of land you've chosen. Train on absolutely anything you'd like to make better. Try lots of rollbacks, loping off 30 feet before abruptly turning back, then repeat, repeat, repeat. Practice your backing, your spins, your speed or gait transitions. The key is to work intensely until the horse WANTS to stand at the spot you picked. After you've tuckered it out a bit, head back to your crossing point and offer the horse a chance to relax a moment, then to move forward.

Teach Your Horse to Lower Its Head While Standing

"Horse, quit playing games with that appaloosa and behave yourself. Drop your head, leave it there, quit antagonizing me."

While plenty of the material contained in this text will either directly or indirectly teach you how to drop your horse's head while you're actively riding, (to travel in a more "collected" frame or to "calm down," for instance), this chapter will show you how to do so while you're standing still. With practice, you should be able to thoroughly teach this exercise to most horses on the planet in under twenty minutes.

There are three reasons you'll want to know this material: One, this is a pretty neat trick and it makes you look really cool. Two, if you're standing around (daisy-chain style) hanging out with your equestrian buds, you'll have a way to tell a mischievous horse "Quit playing games with that appaloosa and behave yourself. Drop your head, leave it there, quit antagonizing me and the appy." Three, you can take this material and extrapolate. Learn this routine at a standstill, mull over what you pick up and try the concepts out while walking, trotting, or loping to shape up a high-headed horse. (Yes, the approach to bringing the horse's head down here is slightly different from the things you might try while moving but the basic ideas are wholly adaptable, given a little thought. Refer to the "Classic Serpentine" and "Softening" chapters for the recommended way to accomplish this while in motion.)

Your goal will be this: When practiced to perfection, you should be able to pick up your reins gingerly with two fingers (like holding a stinky sock) to a height of about two inches—and the horse will drop his head like a rock in a pond. While practicing this you should be thinking of how you can put these concepts to work for you (in whole or in part) when you're riding later.

What you should know about this exercise: If you own a gaited horse, practicing this material may make you think you've broken your horse, and not in a good way. (But you haven't, as I'll explain.) You'll teach the horse to drop his head when you pick up the reins—and at some point, maybe tomorrow, maybe next week, you may find him either carrying it too low because he misunderstands or because he's obnoxiously evading your bit pressure. Regardless of why it happens, (or to whom) remember that it's our release that tells the horse where to carry his head. If you work through this material and suddenly you've got a peanut roller on your hands, simply hold pressure on the reins till the head finds the level you're looking for (what's "natural" for your horse) and release your pressure. (So, nutshell: If you teach this at a standstill, and your horse begins dropping his head incorrectly later while moving, simply hold your pressure until the head is in the right position. Hint: You may need to lock your fists against the saddle to keep the horse from pulling the reins free, giving himself an unwarranted release.)

Hop on your horse, take up your reins with both hands, and apply three pounds of pressure equally on both. (The number of pounds is an approximation, adjust accordingly. Also, it doesn't matter which direction you pull from—your horse simply wants you out of his mouth.) Take up your reins and pause. Now, here's where we try something a little different from our typical training. Most of the time, we want to release the reins when the horse "gives to pressure." Now, however, we want to perform a little reverse psychology. This time I want you to wait and feel for the horse to pull against you.

(If you're saying "What the heck does he mean 'apply x-amount of pressure'? I can't picture that." Yeah, that never made sense to me either—until I realized that your typical coffee can holds about four pounds of feed—and picking up a full can would feel the same as if I applied four pounds of pressure when pulling on something... like the horse's mouth. That's a good way to "picture in your mind" what it should feel like when you pick up the reins. Plus, habitually quantifying the pressure you apply to the reins is a good way to chart your improvement (or the lack thereof) because it tells you whether your horse is progressing or not. If it took four pounds yesterday, it should take less than four today. But... if it's more than four, you'll know objectively that you're doing something wrong. Think back over what you've been doing, tie off your loose ends or try something entirely different.)

So, you're sitting up there, applying three pounds of even pressure to the reins... It may happen in ten seconds or you may find yourself waiting half a minute longer, but (typically) within a minute you should feel the horse pull against you or lower his head. The instant he does either, no matter how slight, you let go. And here's your key to success... when you do release, you must allow the reins to "be pulled from" your hands, (as opposed to "letting go"). When you first begin, and the horse just barely drops his head or pulls against you, you'll need to exaggerate this release by actively dropping your hands while simultaneously allowing the reins to be pulled from your grip. Later, when his head drops further, you can simply allow them to be pulled, dispensing with the exaggerated movement. This is the most important factor, so I'll repeat: You must motivate the horse to actually pull the reins through your hands to gain its release.

A Frequently Asked Question: Will the horse then learn the nasty habit of pulling on the reins? Answer: Yes, briefly. Still, we're counting on that and will use it to our advantage here. We'll know this and be conscious to "go back and fix" this when or if it crops up. Frequently in our training we break one thing while fixing another. I'm sure you've seen that many times yourself. Two steps forward, one back. It can be a challenge, but your horse needs to learn to read your body language, to learn that picking up the reins with you "sitting like so" means one thing—and you picking up the reins "sitting another way" means something else. That's what practice is all about: Push your horse to stop reacting and to start thinking. If you later feel that your horse has begun rudely or incorrectly pulling away, simply hold your pressure till the head is in the correct position AND he releases the pressure you feel through his neck (or, he's "polite").

Another Frequently Asked Question: "How does the horse know to drop his head to his knees while I'm standing here in place and then to only drop it x-amount later when we're riding?" Answer: In time, a combination of factors will tell the horse what you're looking for: 1) The situation. The horse knows you typically ask for such-and-such while hanging out with your friends and something entirely different when rounding a barrel. If you don't think this is true, then why does your horse know to run from the bridle in your hand but toward the feed bucket in your hand? Or to meet you at the gate at feeding time but to run away when you remove the halter? Or where the exit to the arena is or that you always stop loping at Frank's driveway? 2) Your release of rein pressure sends a very strong signal and gives you the ability to put the horse's head at any elevation. Your release says "That's it, right there." 3) Your body position. When you simply concentrate on something, you make small changes in the way you carry your body. Your horse reads this. Whether you're standing or being carried, your horse has nature's gift of reading body language innately.

Tip: As you release the reins, this will go much quicker if you release as if "reverse milking a cow." I'll explain: Put your hand out, making a fist. Now, one finger at a time, open your hand, starting with your pinky and working up toward your index finger. So, as the horse tugs on the reins, you will allow them to be pulled, you'll slightly drop your hands and arms to follow the motion—and finally you'll open your fist, one finger at a time, pinky finger then ring finger then bird finger then, lastly, index finger and thumb. (When you and the horse have learned this exercise, you can dispense with the theatrics and simplify your movements—but the exaggerated actions will help you both communicate to your horse and find a rhythm in the beginning.) This seemingly bizarre tip will cause you to find the timing you need to hurry this particular exercise along. You'll find a similar situation described in the chapter "How to Pick Up Your Reins Like a Pro." You may want to check that out.

If your horse moves backward: Ignore it; don't try to stop him, just allow yourself to be carried and stay focused, waiting for him to pull. He's most likely signaling that he's not "giving to pressure"—but let's not over think this. Horses often try walking backward for awhile. If you ignore it, the horse will stop when it learns that backing doesn't afford a release. Fixing it would complicate matters. (Okay, you may want to try this when he backs up if it's really bugging you: Don't change anything, keep that even pressure on the reins, but if he backs up, try sitting up straight. This changes the tilt of your pelvis and your weight distribution and oftentimes signals to even the most recalcitrant horse that you're not looking for "back." Again, though, the simplest course is to just ignore the back up and let it fade on its own.)

Motivation and expectations: If you're sitting up there, applying your even pressure and nothing happens for a full minute: You're either looking for too much of a drop in the horse's head elevation or too much "pull" from him. Back off your expectations and "release on less." Remember, we want him to pull against us in this case to gain a release—so a horse that is "just hanging out" is almost certainly applying at least a little downward pressure—otherwise his head would be floating. Beyond this, you might hurry things along by consciously finding a way to irritate him enough to MAKE him want to pull away. If your horse seems content to allow you to hang on the reins forever, motivate him by applying more bit pressure (a few more pounds, not fifty). If still nothing, try gently drumming his sides equally with both of your legs. Find a 1-2-3, 1-2-3 beat and stick with it. If still nothing, you can increase the intensity of your thumping, but stay rhythmic. More often than not, you're looking for too much of a change from your horse and need to scale back on "what it takes to get a release."

When you can pick up the two reins, apply even pressure and consistently cause the horse to tug downward, it's a simple thing to repeat the process, asking for more and more and more, until his head will drop to his knees or lower. In the end, he'll be dropping his head not as you actually apply pressure—but when you simply reach for the rein. Accomplishing this, takes a pattern and a sort of "tempo to your training." You know how, when a fly lands on you and you swat him away and several seconds later he's back again and again and again—like clockwork—you know that pattern? That's what you'll replicate here, with a very similar pattern and attitude. (You're the fly.) You take up the reins, he pushes his nose down, you release as if "reverse milking" the cow. Pause a beat. Pick up the reins, egg him on to pull away, release as he does. Each time you do this, ask for one percent more "down with the head" than the time before. If he stalls out or plateaus, respond by thumping his sides (again, at a steady, Indian-dance-tom-tom beat).

When you can pick up the two reins, apply even pressure and cause the horse to reliably drop his head to his knees, begin using just one hand to make your requests. One hand will apply pressure, the other will remain "in the game," helping out the other by giving or taking slack as necessary, but they should no longer apply pressure evenly. (If you continued using your hands together there will come a point when you will not be able to reel out enough slack and your horse will begin over-bending at the poll to avoid your pressure. That is definitely not a position you want to foster.) Note that you can do this entire exercise – start to finish – using one hand if you wish. I suggest two hands from the start because it makes it easier to bring the horse's head back to center should it bring its head across to your boot.

Build from here by making the drop of the head happen fluidly. Horses will usually begin dropping their head, let's say, 12 inches and then hesitate, then maybe another 8 inches and hesitate again. Make the whole movement fluid by giving the horse a slight release of pressure (as a reward) as it begins to drop, but hold the reins in your hand till he hesitates, then add a small amount of pressure back to say "Keep going." Release fully only when the head drops to where you want it (and he's polite about it).

Finally, when you can pick up the two reins, apply even pressure and cause the horse to fluidly drop his head, you'll want to consciously "add a cue to" your request. When you apply pressure, you're applying motivation. "I'll let go when you do something." In the same way that touching your horse's back right flank can be your cue for a left lead departure (a cue, not a motivator), you simply picking up your reins in two fingers should become your horse's cue in this exercise. How do you get there? By progressively asking the horse to work on less. Actually work at using less and less pressure with each try, seeing if you can't wean your horse off "being made to do it." If he slips back in his training (let's say in the next day or so), then just fall back to a point where he's really nailing it and work forward. Practice this exercise and you'll be amazed at how simply grasping the reins lightly in two fingers causes the horse to drop his head. (It'll amaze your friends, I promise you that.)

Better Back Ups

If you've practiced the "Clockwork Exercise," specifically and successfully teaching your horse to step on "6 o'clock" repeatedly, then your horse can and will back up for you today. What we'll do here then is work to make the movement smoother and quicker.

The key to effectively teaching back ups is to cue the horse and get it into a proper frame before asking for the back up itself. The trained horse will read your body language and prompts, know what's coming, and quickly prepare himself. The younger horse must first be "framed up" by you. If you've felt a horse drag though its back up, its legs splayed out, its back dropped and head high in the air, you've felt a horse that is not "framed up" to back up.

Optimally, a horse should use the same correct "posture" walking backward as he uses (or should use) to walk forward, his belly up and back rounded, his head at a respectable height, the back legs carried a practical distance from the front legs. (The same "posture" but not the same foot pattern. When backing, his feet fall in the same pattern as when he trots, with the right front moving with the left rear and vice versa.) In teaching the back up, then, you must do what it takes to get your horse in a soft and correct, "moving forward" position BEFORE YOU EVEN ASK HIM TO BACK AND THROUGHOUT HIS TRANSITION FROM FORWARD TO BACKWARD.

We'll begin by relaxing the horse to our reins and requests: Start from a standstill with loose reins—and that means NO PRESSURE on the horse's mouth; you need to see a pronounced droop in the reins as you begin to move forward. Start with loose reins and trot forward, then pick up the left rein and apply pressure as you ask for a circle to the left, release your pressure when the horse drops his head or softens his neck. Go forward two strides (not one, not three) and ask for the same to the right. Practice this one billion times or until your horse has become soft from withers to nose tip, whichever happens first.

With your horse good and relaxed and bending, trot forward on droopy reins for a few beats before picking one up and asking the horse to disengage. (Disengaging, as we've been practicing, puts the horse into a shape more conducive to backing up. It makes him stand more upright, brings the back legs up under his body, and energizes him, sort of like compressing a spring.) Try picking up the right rein and ask the hips to move to their left. The instant the horse steps its hips across, lessen your pressure and ask the horse to move forward. Move forward just a step or two before saying out loud "Step on 6 o'clock" and then use your right rein to ask any one of the four feet to do just that. (You want constant motion: Forward, disengage, forward, back.)

It's a lot like parallel parking on the streets of Chicago: You back in, then correct your wheels and pull forward till you hit the guy in front of you, then go backward till you hit the car behind you. There is very little pause between each maneuver and soon you're parked. In this chapter, keep the parking analogy in your head and never "keep asking" your horse to back up if he loses his "forward-going posture" as he backs. In that case, forget "back" and get movement of any kind before circling back to your original request.

If your horse begins to back up, release your reins after just a step or two and scoot forward with energy. Ride and relax for a few beats before repeating the sequence.

If your horse insists on pushing forward rather than back (because in the horse's experience, that's all you've ever asked for), disengage his back feet, bring your reins back toward your belly button, then try again. This is just a matter of supplying motivation and waiting till your horse figures out what you want. Keep telling yourself, "He can only go six directions and I've got all but one shut off...." If your horse remains confused, fall back to practicing "3s," then "4s," then "5s" and finally "6s" with the clockwork exercise as previously outlined.

If your horse balks and freezes up, bump its sides if you think it might help dislodge the feet. If the bumping doesn't get you moving in very short order, don't allow it to park out. Immediately boost the horse forward several steps then ask the shoulder to stop and the hips to swing, (in any direction). When the shoulder stops and the hips swing, release a bit of the pressure and then bring your reins to the area directly above the point of the horse's shoulder—the left "cup," were it wearing a brassiere—and keep that pressure till the horse takes a step backward—or even leans back. If you become stalemated, move forward and disengage, then drop your pressure altogether and try to back up again. Repeat the entire sequence until the moment the horse lifts a leg to step back then release your pressure entirely, scoot forward with verve, and pet the horse.

Keep going over this exercise, building on small changes, until you can pick up a single rein and the horse will stop dead and begin to back. (Then mirror what you've just practiced with your other rein.)

When you can get the horse to back up a step or two consistently, get a third step by simply keeping your pressure steady, bumping with both legs evenly if you need a bit of motivation and then dropping your pressure and moving forward following that third step. Don't ask for two steps one minute, thirty-two steps the next. Build to it over time.

2 Tips: 1) As you train for greater distance, remember to only let your pressure up when the horse is speeding up, never ever when he's slowing down. If necessary, bump with both legs to momentarily speed up, release, and move forward. Your timing in that respect has everything to do with your success here. Your release is a reward: Don't reward the horse for moving slower. 2) If your horse turns into a great giant slug, trot around for awhile, put some energy back into the moment, then go back to backing. Or, try backing at an angle by turning the hips as you've learned. Backing at an angle forces the horse to put feet in the same spot occupied by other feet—so they learn to raise their knees higher—which translates to a quicker, lighter back up.

In the above sequence, picking up your droopy reins serves as a pre-cue (saying "Yo, a request is coming"), seconds later you bring your reins toward your belly button to cue for a back up, and then, should the horse ignore your request to back up, you apply motivation, either disengaging if it freezes or bumping with your legs if it moves too slowly. The sequence is important: Were you to simply ride around with constant pressure on the reins, you'd soon burn out your cue. If you bumped randomly, the bumps would soon mean nothing. The cues are essential: Like the needle on your car's gas gauge that says "Think about getting gas," you gotta tell the horse something's coming in order for him to prepare. Without your gas gauge, you'd be walking; without the cues your horse won't be in position to back up when asked to do so.

To really take this to the next level, try the following: At a walk, with both reins in your hands, experiment with "tilting" your pelvis or sinking your butt deeper into the seat or moving your legs just a hair forward or bringing the reins just a hair back or all of the above… to see what tiny, tiny, tiny bit of communication you can use to get your horse to successfully stop and back up. Experiment. Practice parallel parking with the lightest cues you can imagine. Teach a cue so light that a friend on the ground wouldn't even see it.

Simple Steps to Power Steering

We'll use what you learned in the Clockwork Exercise to firmly ingrain in your brain the importance of being specific with your requests—and we'll see how that precision can be used to turn on a dime and ride circles that don't look like eggs.

Prerequisite chapters: the "Clockwork Exercise," "Neck Reining How-To" and "Train Your Horse to Travel Straight."

How many times have you asked your horse to turn, only to look down and see that you're not turning so much as "veering"? You think "right" and turn your horse's head to the right but you change direction like a plane being blown off course?

To get spot-on circles and turns, you'll first need to think a bit differently. No longer will you aim your horse and hope for the best. No longer will you simply ask your horse to "turn right." From now on, it's "put your foot exactly there, at that angle and do it with your very next step." Anything less is unacceptable. If you ask for a precise, 30 degree turn with the very next step, shuffling loosely over at 12 degrees is just not cutting it.

What you will quickly find is that horse training is easier—not harder—for you and your horse when you're precise and objective with your requests. Stop. Really consider that last sentence; it's what you're learning here today; it's how you'll attack the lesson which follows. "Training is easier—not harder—for you and your horse when you're precise and objective with your requests." You'll do your horse no favors when you release the rein when "he's almost got it"—something which holds true in all aspects of your training.

Bearing in mind that if a guy or gal can't steer their horse, they haven't got much of a horse, let's see how you do in that department: Mount up, pick out a rock and trot a circle around it. Steer as you would normally.

Next: Circle that same rock—but once you initially lift your rein and suggest "turn," leave the rein exactly in that place and don't move it again unless you step off course. Get back on your line, then immediately put your guiding hand back into place and freeze it there. You don't ask your horse to trot, then say "trot, trot, trot" repeatedly to keep your horse trotting. Nor should you have to steer and steer and steer to keep moving on a truly round circle (or a straight line, for that matter). Ideally, your horse should read this simple rein cue from you, couple it with experience and the rest of your body language (how you sit, your weight placement, etcetera), and turn through a perfectly round circle—without constant, changing, guidance from the reins.

(Note: Do your testing with a snaffle bit. Outfitting your horse like Anthony Hopkins in "Silence of the Lambs" with 600lbs of leverage bits, tie-downs and miscellaneous hardware will make you feel more accomplished, but it's not a fair test.)

Afterward, compare the first set of trips around the rock to the second. Do you see by comparison that your horse requires more guidance than you might have thought?

Were your circles truly round? Or did you drift in and out and make constant course corrections? Ideally, your horse would have stayed "between the reins" and not drifted—but, if we rode a lopsided circle or found ourselves frequently steering back onto our line, it may be that we've been kidding ourselves about the maneuverability of our horse. We don't have the control we thought we did and need to dial in our training.

To perfect our steering, we'll begin by very briefly refreshing ourselves on the Clockwork Exercise. Very specifically, I want you to trot for exactly twenty intense minutes, never stopping in that time. No talking to your friends, no bathroom breaks, no joy riding. As you move, pick up the right rein, apply pressure, look down and pick a spot to the right and slightly in front of your horse, (that is, one or two o'clock to the right, ten or eleven o'clock to your left). Hold your pressure until the horse steps exactly onto that spot. The moment he does, drop your rein and pet your horse. Trot off only as far as it takes to compose yourself and take a very quick break, then repeat, varying the numbers you request. Make sure that you relax your posture and put a droopy bow into those reins between repetitions. It's critical that you signal to your horse after each repetition that "That's all I wanted, that step right there." (If you don't relax between reps, he'll think it's a twenty minute exercise and turn you off. It's not, it's a simple step followed by a release.)

If you've nailed the full spectrum of the Clockwork Exercise, this should be a piece of cake. If you have trouble, remember, he can only go 6 directions (including up and down), so motivating him by applying pressure to the rein (and bumping when necessary) will cause him to guess, searching for a release. Your timing will tell the horse "Yes, that's what I wanted." With a bit of consistent practice he'll be routinely stepping where and when you want.

Afterward, relax for exactly twenty minutes. Then, ride for another twenty solid minutes. This time, I want you to go back to circling that rock. Put a pronounced droop in your reins and ask the horse to circle. Use only the lightest of pressure on your rein to steer and allow the horse to make mistakes, to drift off his line. When it does, pick up your rein and put that front foot back onto the line, back onto "1" or "2," "10" or "11." After you make each correction, put your body back into a more neutral position, continuing to follow the line of travel with your eyes, your reins hanging down.

Do not use your legs to cue the horse to turn. At this stage you only use your legs to tell the horse to move. Your reins say which direction. If your horse stops trotting, use your legs to ask him to move. If your horse doesn't turn correctly, use your rein to tell him exactly where to move.

The trick to this: EVERY FOURTH TIME that you must make a correction, change the angle with which you hold your rein and ask the hip to take several steps sideways (as you learned back in the chapter "Hip Control, Part II"). You can use one or both of two angles to make this happen: Either bring your right hand toward your left shoulder (bringing the horse's nose toward yours like you're steer wrestling) or bring your right hand toward the horse's right hip (bringing the horse's nose toward his right hip). Apply a tad more pressure when needed and concentrate on holding the rein till the hip takes a couple of steps across.

Remember: Your horse will only get better if you allow him to make mistakes—so be very, very careful to use less and less rein, less and less pressure.

Now, when you work on perfecting your circles, correct your horse when he begins to drift in or out by picking up the rein and "placing the foot" where it should be. Motivate your horse to stay on its line by swinging those hips (the horse's) every fourth time it veers off course. They don't want to have to swing their rears across because of the extra energy involved, so they learn that it's easiest to simply walk "straight" on a curve. With practice, they'll begin doing just that.

Diagonal Movement ("Leg Yields Without the Legs")

What you'll achieve here: Smooth and easy diagonal lines of travel plus a "polite" horse that moves fluidly from a walk to a trot to a canter on the lightest of cues. What you'll fix: Horses that want to leap into and speed through their transitions, horses that ignore our cues, horses that just trod along "going through the motions."

Prerequisite training: You'll need the ability to move your horse's hips and shoulders independently, (refer to the chapters "Hip Control, Part I"; "Hip Control, Part II," "Shoulder Control," "The Clockwork Exercise" and "Softening").

"Lateral movement" means that some part of your horse (maybe the whole animal) is moving to the side. That's all it means: "To the side." Some lateral movements are relatively simple (like the side pass), while others are more advanced, requiring fancier footwork and greater degrees of collection, balance, timing and experience (like haunches-in and haunches out, the half pass and shoulder-in). All sideways movements take plenty of wet saddle blankets to perfect as your horse slowly learns to carry the two of you while developing the necessary muscle and flexibility.

We're "basically training" your horse - so now we'll learn "leg yielding" (though that term as used here is a misnomer because we won't be using our legs as you'll soon learn). "Leg yielding" is when the horse moves forward at an angle chosen by you, his body straight except for his head which is tipped just slightly away from the direction in which he travels, (he looks one way, moves another). Move entirely sideways (90 degrees) and that leg yield is called a "side pass" or "full pass." (You learned to side pass with the "Clockwork Exercise" though you can improve what you've got with the work in this chapter.)

Practically speaking, you teach these things because you want to open and close gates and show off to your friends. But you also invest the time because it improves your horse's balance, flexibility, muscling and overall ability to carry you around. You'll improve its attitude as it learns to work with you and you'll get better turns, better lope departures, better rollbacks, better turns around a barrel, better just fill-in-the-blank anything. Teaching these things gives your horse a greater ability to do anything and everything.

You will not use your legs in the training which follows because your reins offer a stronger, cleaner signal that your horse is less likely to ignore. Further, your legs will only serve to irritate a horse in an early stage of training. (Go poke somebody in the ribs, completely out of the blue, and see how they react.) Leg pressure can always be added in later-stage training to offer yet another source of communication. Today, we're keeping things simple, so your reins tell direction, your legs tell speed. Period. (Refer to the upcoming chapter, curiously entitled "Reins Tell Direction, Legs Tell Speed," for more on this.)

The steps we will ask the horse to take aren't necessarily hard for him. Granted, it takes time to build necessary muscle—but for the most part what makes our training a challenge is the resistance he naturally throws up. When first asking for lateral movement, he'll tense up and resist because traveling to that tree over there with his hips and shoulders out of kilter just doesn't add up. It makes no sense. Our job is to communicate and foster a benevolent dictatorship, making him understand through repetition that he can and should do what is asked—and that life is easy when he travels in a particular fashion, that you'll drop your pressure and "stay out of his mouth."

You will find rather quickly that your horse will travel nicely in one direction and drag his shoulders or hips-in the other. That's normal—in fact, look for it in order to learn from it. Ask yourself "If Dobber travels so great to the right, why is he so lousy traveling to the left? What's different?" Travel the good direction and make a mental note of how he carries his head, neck, shoulders, belly, and hips. Up? Down? Upright or dropped and sagging? Soft? Rigid? Pushing against your leg or bent away? What you'll undoubtedly find is that (in the good direction), he keeps his hips lined up directly behind his shoulders which are raised. But go the opposite direction and you'll find the hip dragging and sluggish, the shoulder may lean and move at best begrudgingly. You'll feel more like you're turning than moving diagonally. Make a "muscle memory note" of what feels right, then later see what it takes to achieve that same body positioning going the other way. It's all the same to the horse—so if you don't care, he certainly won't.

The good new is, your horse has only got two "ends," the front and back, and we can take advantage of this: If the front is too far to the left, we can move the shoulder to the right or we can move the hip to the left. If he won't move his darn shoulder, we can get the same result (a straight horse) by moving his hip. That's two ways to fix the same thing, to realign our horse. (If he was shaped like a triangle we'd be in trouble.) So keep this in mind as you practice this material. Don't have a cow if you can't get a hip moved; if the shoulders move easier, fix your alignment with them instead. If one door's closed, try another.

The exercise you'll practice here, in a nutshell, is simply this: You will ask your horse to transition (from a walk to a trot, from a trot to a walk, from a trot to a lope, from the lope back to the trot)—but only when he's traveling at an angle. That's it!

Why the diagonal transitions? Because if your horse impolitely plods ahead and pushes through his transitions, what he's doing is lining up the bones in his body and, once "stacked" in such a way, he can easily bull through any pressure you might apply through the reins. We've all felt this: We ask for the lope and the horse moves into it with all the grace of a jackhammer. By asking for the sideways movement, we're causing the horse to keep his body slightly curved as it moves ahead into the next gait, retaining for us the ability to "adjust" certain body parts like when we move the hip to the right or the shoulders to the left.

For the same reason, use just the one rein—and do not cheat. Cheating here, by using two reins, again causes the horse to line his body up and go rigid, rather than keeping his body somewhat arched. This would make your goal (of relaxed travel) completely impossible. Don't do that. Do what it takes to guide the horse with a single rein. (Your "off" hand "helps out" where needed, reeling out and taking up slack. Be careful that it's not in any way calling the shots or applying pressure. Refer to the chapter "How to Pick Up Your Reins Like a Pro" for guidance, specifically the section on one-handed rein handling.)

Here's what you'll do: As you ride forward (begin first at a walk), pick up one rein and ask the horse to move diagonally. Keep the lateral movement and gradually increase your speed into the jog. Release your rein, ride directly forward and reward your horse: Exercise completed. After releasing your rein, travel forward only as far as it takes for you to relax momentarily on that rein, telling the horse "That's all I wanted, thanks." Then pick the rein back up and ask for diagonal movement as you simultaneously slow back to a walk. The direction you "go up" and then "come back down" doesn't matter—though I strongly suggest that you find a rhythm ("Up and to the right twice, back down to the left every other time," whatever) because counting keeps you objective. Objectivity keeps you proactive as opposed to reactive—and calling the shots is always better than reacting to what the horse throws at you.

If you and your horse are new to this concept of riding diagonally, it's really just a matter of keeping your eyes ahead on the diagonal line you'd like to follow, then first asking the hips to step onto that line, then the shoulders or vice versa. Then, while traveling, you keep your horse moving diagonally by adjusting either the front or back end individually as needed. (Refer back to the previous, corresponding chapters on hip and shoulder movement for guidance.) In this particular rendition, you simply ask for this while stepping on the gas. Walk forward and ask for speed as you ask the hips to move across then ask the shoulders to step across onto your diagonal line. Trot directly forward a few beats, then slow back to a walk, again at an angle, using the same fixes. Before long, the horse will begin to anticipate and he'll bring both front and back over at the same time.

The trick to this specific exercise is in the timing of your release. (Releasing when the horse relaxes teaches the horse to stay "easy" through his transition. In turn, that gives us the benefits listed above.) It's also in the horse's innate ability to anticipate. It doesn't take long for him to realize that you'll release your rein pressure when he travels at an angle and picks up the lope and within a short period of time, he'll do both of those things when you simply reach for the rein. The best part is that you don't have to put the horse into some cockeyed position to pick up the lope—he assumes a position natural to him—so your transition looks smooth and effortless.

The first few times you do this, you can release when the horse simply moves diagonally through his transition. He moves diagonally and begins trotting while doing so, you release the rein, done. However, after you've done this several times, and the horse has the concept of "We start or stop trotting ONLY as we move diagonally," then begin "not releasing" until you're moving diagonally, you've made your transition AND you feel some softness (that is, a relaxation) from the horse's neck or body. Keep your energy up; keep the horse moving diagonally; keep him aware that "something is expected."

When you begin—on the average horse who can already move his shoulders and hips as prescribed—what you'll find is this: You can get the movement—but the horse is testy. Or stiff. Or he lumbers through his transitions. Or he anticipates (not in a good way). He'll carry the hip way out here or the shoulder way over there. It'll feel clunky. You'll find yourself using the second rein (again, a big no-no). You'll start and stop with hesitations between the movements and move with all the grace of rusty gate. Ignore all these things and keep at it. Keep focused on your objective which is simply to get the horse to transition only when moving diagonally and don't release the rein until he relaxes. Keep things simple: If the shoulders drag, move them over. If the hips drag, move them over. It's not complicated; it's one or the other. What matters is that you keep your eye on the ball, keep with it, and stay consistent. Practice intensely for twenty minutes, take twenty minutes off and repeat. Do this for several days and you'll be amazed at the control you'll build.

Challenges you might face:

1) If you've completed the diagonal or transition—and the horse just won't soften his grip on the rein—and seconds are ticking by—just drop the rein and try the whole thing again going the opposite direction. (Alternatively, you could also ask for a disengagement of the hip using that same rein—that's another good fix.) What you don't want to happen is to simply ride around, waiting and waiting for the horse to relax, allowing him to "get used to" hanging on the bit. You're better off dropping the rein entirely and starting over on the other side. Also, remember to look for very small improvements and build on them.

2) Horses tend to become more energetic through this exercise. If your horse gets too "amped," do serpentines to calm him down or look to the chapters "Slow Down, Part I" & "Slow Down, Part II."

3) If your horse chronically drags his hip to the inside, cure this by spending the next few training sessions insisting that it actually lead through the movement. That is, insist that your horse bring the hip not straight behind the shoulders, but have that hip really lead the shoulder by several inches. Getting that hip "better than it needs to be" will cause the horse to carry it properly at more relaxed times because he'll become more accustomed to really reaching with that back leg. It also casts you in the role of "proactive" rather than "reactive" rider.

4) Often you can get a hip moved properly into line, but that shoulder just doesn't want to move on a diagonal path as quickly, resulting in a horse that moves "at an angle to the angle." The hip will be perfect but the shoulder drags. To tell that shoulder to hurry up and get in front of the hips, keep your grip on that indirect rein in order to keep the neck somewhat bent and the head tipped slightly away from the direction of travel, but ease up a tad on the pressure. Simultaneously raise your other hand and add pressure with a direct rein. Do as you did in the Clockwork Exercise to ask the shoulder to step across using primarily that direct rein, the left hand says "nine," the right says "three." When the horse gets the idea, drop the direct rein in favor of the indirect. Note that when any part of the horse drags, it often helps to speed the horse up a notch.

Now, here's something you'll find yourself doing—and YOU SHOULD NOT: You will look at something ahead of you like the gate and attempt to move diagonally relative to the gate. Instead of moving diagonally, however, your horse may simply turn—and you'll suddenly be facing away from the gate. As a human, the natural thing to do would be to stop, point the horse back toward the gate, and start over—but don't do it. Remember the bottom line here is simply to get diagonal steps. If you find your horse veering off, don't line him back up—just keep asking for that diagonal step. Lining him back up will cause you to make about half a dozen corrections that only serve to muddy the waters.

On a related note, here's something to be concerned about: Quite often riders think they're moving diagonally—when in fact, they're simply turning. Guard against this by laying down a rope, walking along it a few feet (or a shadow)—and then watch to make sure that both sets of legs (front and back) move off that rope diagonally—as opposed to turning (front then back) away and off the rope. Try this simple solution once and you'll see exactly how it makes things crystal clear.

Practice this exercise until the horse begins to read your mind. The first day you practice, it'll be clunky. By the third or fourth day you'll be amazed at how the horse actually begins to move in a relaxed fashion into a trot from a walk or slows to a trot from a lope... as you pick up the rein, almost as you think it. This anticipation is a good thing. It's what you're looking for and a process you should cultivate as a horse trainer. The two of you have begun to look like a team.

Softening

Get your horse giving to the bit, dropping its head and rounding its body, rather than bracing when you pick up the reins. Being "rounded" is the crux of collection. Collection gives us a horse that can readily follow our requests with lightness and precision with zero hesitation.

Prerequisite: The "parallel parking" that you did in the "Better Back Ups" chapter also goes a long way toward softening your horse, specifically through its directional transitions (when going forward to backward) and transitioning between gaits.

If you were to take a stout metal rod and press one end against a nearby wall, the only way your hand (holding the opposite end) can get any closer to the wall would be for that rod to skid up, down, left or right there where it was first placed against the wall. When a horse is "pressed against the bit" - and reacts by stiffening throughout his entire body - he is that unyielding metal rod "pressed against the wall." (His tail doesn't get any closer to his chin.) He also turns like garbage, blows his lead departures and wins no awards for attitude, performance, or symmetry. He's slow to carry out our requests and, depending on his mood and the day he's had, he might also buck, bolt or rear.

By contrast, if you took a metal spring and pressed it against the wall, your hand would get closer to the wall as the spring bows upwards. Also, and importantly, the head of the spring would stay where it was placed on the wall, just as we want our horse's head to stay where "placed against" the bit when we pick up the reins—this, as opposed to jutting it's chin out and away or thrusting it's head up or down. It should "bow" (rhymes with "snow") through it's body, (the back going up, the back legs getting closer to the front legs) just as the spring. Here, we'll train the horse to "give" (mentally and physically) in just such a manner. Putting the "spring in our horse" gives us a horse that can act on our commands in an immediate, willing, and controlled, manner.

To accomplish this, our horses must learn to "round up" their bodies. Being "rounded" is the core of collection, something called for often in future, advanced training. "Collected horses" travel with their backs and bellies raised, heads tucked, and back legs closer to their front legs. Think "giant furry ball." Collection gives us a horse that can readily—and immediately—follow our requests with lightness and precision. With zero hesitation it can "rollll" right, rollll left, rollll sideways. By definition, it's a horse ready to do a rider's bidding fluidly and straight away. We won't achieve true and lasting "collection" with this simple exercise, but we will introduce the concept.

Step One, ask the horse to "soften" while standing still: Get on your horse and, standing still, take up both reins evenly. Apply light pressure, perhaps three or four pounds, as you simultaneously drop both legs against your horse with the weight of "two wet towels." (Many methods of horse training call for momentary leg pressure to signal to the horse that he'll need to "round up" for whatever he's about to be asked to do. We might as well get in that habit here.) Let your legs fall back to where gravity dictates but keep your hold on the reins, feeling for your horse to soften through his poll and/or neck, however slightly, and then release. Actually feeling the horse relax through the reins is what you release on when you first begin – not any particular head or neck position. You could keep your eyes closed throughout this entire procedure, were you of a mind to do so. It's all about what you're feeling. This is because your horse can carry his head at an acceptable level—while keeping the muscles involved rock solid – and that stiffness would seriously retard performance. Softness – that is to say a certain measure of relaxation – signals a willingness more than any particular angle or head position, so there's our means to an end.

While head positioning isn't something we'll be overly concerned with here as we start, if his head shoots up or hits the ground obnoxiously, simply hold your pressure till he has his head at the angle you'd ride with—and you feel a little softening—then release. If he backs, drop your pressure altogether on one rein and use the other to ask him to move his hips over. Keep your pressure steady through this and, when he's stopped, take the reins back in both hands until he gives. (Remember to keep even pressure throughout that fix. Your horse should not feel you add, then drop, then add pressure. Releasing in the middle gives him an unwarranted release and reward.) If time ticks by, let's say 40 seconds, with no softening from your horse, try first picking up a single rein and applying pressure to get a bend in the neck, then add pressure with that second rein. That will often cause a horse to drop or relax his head a bit. Still nothing? Repeatedly disengage, turning the horse's rear end around a planted front shoulder. After a few minutes, maybe ten or twenty, you'll find a decidedly more obliging horse. Repetitively isolating and turning the back end is a great way to soften the front end.

Step Two, ask the horse to "soften" briefly while moving at a walk: When you can get the horse to relax through the reins at a complete standstill, the next step is to do the same while walking. Pick up the reins, bring them an inch or two forward (away from your belly button) and ask the horse to walk forward. It is critical that you are not applying any pressure to the reins when you ask the horse to move off at this stage. There should be a very pronounced "droop" in the reins as the horse begins to move. Asking your horse to move off while simultaneously holding pressure through the reins is all well and good when you have a reason to do so, as you'll soon see. However, it's not good when we absentmindedly hang on the reins; it's kinda-sorta like driving your car with the brakes on. I've written the steps here in this fashion to break many riders of this habit because I see it time and time again. To see a lasting change in our horse, we must first change ourselves.

So, from a standstill, you'll walk off. A few beats later, you'll drop your legs briefly against the horse's sides (remember, like "two wet towels"), then pick up both reins and apply pressure, asking the horse to soften slightly as you continue to move forward. Release when you get your "give" but keep walking. Praise and pet your horse but do not stop!

From this point forward, do what it takes to ensure that your horse does not hesitate or slow the tempo of his feet even slightly when you pick up the reins and apply pressure as you walk about. And when I say "even slightly," I mean you don't want to feel a muscle twitch or feel a foot drag or feel a change through the reins. It's natural for a horse to slow when we pick up the reins—and it's especially likely when we pick them up and apply some pressure. But this inclination is what we are purposely working to overcome: Henceforth, when you pick up those reins and apply pressure, you need to do what it takes to teach your horse that he is to give to bit pressure AND to keep moving fluidly with no change in tempo whatsoever.

Accomplishing this can be a puzzle—you'll have to stay sharp. If you pick up the reins and apply pressure—and he slows down or puts increased pressure on the bit—then you need to immediately correct this, holding your pressure steady, but bumping with your legs (for instance) to get him back to speed, releasing when he softens and "flows." Now more than ever, you'll really need to work with your horse.

Try it again. You're not steering or stopping and starting at this point; you're just wandering around, picking up the reins and asking for a brief give before dropping them, pausing and repeating. Adjust your timing, pressure, angle, seat, anything and everything, to keep the same even tempo from the time you pick up the reins until he "gives" and you release.

(Question: How can you pick up the reins and stop the horse later—or control it at all, for that matter—if you've taught him to keep moving as just described? Answer: Your total body language. Without even knowing you're doing it, you will carry your body and reins entirely differently when expecting the horse to trot or turn or whatever then you do when you're thinking "stop." I train horses on their basics for a very long time before working on a real, quality stop—and somehow

I manage to get off the horse each evening. Your horse doesn't want to work—he wants to get back to his hay and buddies—so more often than not, you don't have to worry about him figuring out when it's okay to stop. He's real motivated to figure this one out for himself.)

How much are we looking to "pull in" the horse's nose? As your horse learns to give, he'll undoubtedly begin bringing his chin in toward his chest. Generally speaking, if you can get the horse to bring his chin to within five or six inches of his body, that's great at this stage. (You'll find that this very positioning will help your horse move his shoulders more readily left and right, so there are additional payoffs to this.) Note, however, that you absolutely do not want to ask for the head to come in much closer than that. That space between the horse's chin and his chest are, effectively, your brake pads. Should the horse learn the habit of carrying his chin in against his chest, you'll have effectively burned out much control—and man, is it tough to rebuild that "brake pad." Just be wary and don't make more work for yourself in this area; release your pressure when his head is correct.

Every second that you are not actively asking the horse to stop, turn or soften up, those reins should be down, applying zero pressure to your horse's mouth. If you realize that, out of habit, you haven't released the reins in twenty minutes, then start forcing yourself to put one hand on your thigh and the other on top of the reins there on the horse's neck when you are not actually requesting something of the horse. Have a friend watch you to make sure you don't cheat. This will force you to find a more relaxed rhythm; your horse will thank you for the effort.

Step Three, ask the horse to "soften" briefly while trotting: When you can successfully ask your horse to soften at a standstill and then while walking, teach this at a trot. Remember, increasing speed also stokes emotions so don't go out making harsh demands, keep thinking your way through this. Try circling and asking him to drop or soften with one hand (using that same "direct rein" you're using to turn) before adding pressure with the second hand if you're having difficulty beginning right off with two hands. Keep telling yourself that your horse should be calmer at the end of your training than at the start if you want them to remember anything—and if you see him getting progressively more amped, dial things down a notch. We're about to drop back to a walk for the next step so if you're having trouble with this at a faster clip, skip to the next portion, then come back to the trot.

Step Four, begin walking from a standstill with pressure on the reins. Do the following: From a standstill, take up two reins and apply pressure, wrapping and releasing your legs. Ask the horse to soften through its neck and poll – and when it does, ask it to move into a walk. Release your pressure "when you even think the horse is thinking" of taking that very first step while relaxed. If you lose that softness as the horse lifts into that first step (and that's highly likely at first), hold till you do get the softness then release, stop, and try again. Remember, this is about getting and keeping your horse relaxed through the actual transition.

Step Five, stop walking with pressure on the reins: Get the horse to stay soft on the reins as he moves into a walk, drop your pressure when he does, and walk *three steps before asking your horse to soften and stop. Stop the horse by applying even pressure, bringing the reins back an inch, and simply stop riding. Keep up your rein pressure through the stop and really focus on whether or not you feel zero-resistance through that rein as you come to a stop. If your horse comes to a stop and stays soft (for just half an instant), then release your reins fully, praise, and pet. Drop your reins entirely for a few beats and relax before taking them up again and starting over. If your horse resists "softening up," employ any of the tips you've been given so far.

*Traveling three steps in between stops and starts keeps you objective—and it absolutely forces you to test yourself and to learn to be prepared. When you're first learning, give yourself a break and concentrate on just learning the moves. But know that you need to pick an objective number of steps to step (three is what I use) to see the most progress. Trust me here; it'll keep you focused.

In the short time you are walking, it is very important that you put down those reins, however briefly. Force yourself to put one hand on a thigh and hold the reins down on the horse's neck with the other. Relax your body, allowing yourself to be "packed around" or carried. Were you to keep pressure on the horse's mouth (however slight) when you should be "relaxing," your horse will see no break and think that you expect him to memorize a twenty minute dance routine. This simple added step (the quick break) will also make a huge change in the typical rider's ability to communicate and the success they see in their training. Once they (and by "they" I mean "you") build up their "muscle memory," once they can do these moves by rote, they can drop the theatrics and carry themselves more naturally.

Now, it's not all that tough to wrestle his forehead more "onto the vertical" and walk off or come to a stop. What takes true horsemanship, is to get the horse to step off or stop while his head remains relaxed and you're not forcing things. It can be trying, because over and over you'll get that softness and ask for the step, and the horse will immediately "blow it" by pulling on the reins or move haltingly or brace through his neck as he takes that first step. But that's exactly what we're working to fix, so be patient and just keep at it. Experiment—a lot. Try getting "less" softness and "thump thumping" with your legs as you kiss the horse to move off. Try more or less pressure. Try using one rein to get the head bent and soft—then adding that second hand just as the horse picks up that first step. You can even try "locking his head down" by leveraging your fists down behind the pommel of your saddle, then goose him forward in an effort to simply plant the idea, (but know that if you continue in this way he'll never step off lightly). That actual moment of transition is key, but getting it resistance-free can be a real challenge. It's a balancing act.

Step Six, keep the horse soft as you transition from a walk to a trot, then from a trot to a stop: When you can keep your horse feeling soft and relaxed with his forehead perpendicular to the ground as you do your walking transitions, take it up a notch. Practice your "walk-to-trot" and "trot-to-walk" transitions: At a walk, with the reins "dropped," pick up the reins and ask the horse to soften and bring his forehead "more vertical." When he does, ask for him to lift into a trot and release your reins. Trot three steps before asking him to soften and stay relaxed as you come to a walk. Repeat until well-practiced and then practice transitioning from a trot to a full stop. All the previous provisos pertain: Your goal is to feel absolutely no change in tempo or pressure through the reins. (For what it's worth, if you see this as a riddle or brainteaser to be solved, it can actually be kinda fun.)

Step Seven, keep the horse soft as you transition from a trot to a lope: You're undoubtedly noticing the pattern here and can see where to go from here: Get softness as you lift from a trot into a lope just as you did for the slower gaits. If you have had trouble with your horse picking up the wrong lead or exploding into the canter, then know that practicing your trot-to-lope transitions as described will go a long way to affecting a cure. (In fact, practicing your lead departures period will go farther to train your horse "how to canter" than "just cantering" will. If you're training a young horse to canter, for instance, practice plenty of transitions because he'll learn his cadence and balance faster than simply cantering around and around.) If you've set up your horse repeatedly for a correct canter departure only to have it jump off on the wrong lead, you know how exasperating this can be. Think back and you'll know that you lost control in the moment of your transition. Here, you're gaining the ability to control the very instant things go phlooey. Your horse isn't going to leap into the incorrect lead if you have softness and control during your transition.

If you'll steadily work at this, following the steps outlined above, you'll produce a horse whose "body parts" remain under control—but at the same time, they're energized, ready to trot or lope off when given the cue by you. See it this way: You know how, when you're sitting at a traffic light and you're five cars back and the guy who's first isn't paying attention and sits there when the light changes to green? You're ready to go, he isn't. And maybe he's ready—but the lady directly in front of you is on the phone. Again, you're ready, another car isn't. If any car in front of you is not ready to move out, regardless of which one, you're blocked and not going anywhere without a wreck. In my mind, the benefit of the work you've done is in getting all the horse's body parts ready ("energized" and positioned) to move out when the rider gives the green light just like those cars sitting at the intersection.

Getting Leads

Teaching any horse to pick up the correct lead is ninety percent "softening" through its transitions. The rest is "positioning."

Prerequisite: The preceding chapters "Softening" and "Diagonal Movement"

Note: Throughout this training I'll use the words "lope" and "canter" interchangeably. Both terms refer to the same gait, but some schools of thought teach that the canter is more of a collected affair, the western lope more relaxed and "reaching." In our basic training, the difference is negligible.

Position your horse to step off properly—keep it relaxed through the transition—and nine times out of ten you'll get—and keep—the correct lead. Practice those lift-offs again and again—and sooner rather than later, you will have a horse that nails every departure from a simple cue.

In time, you will teach your horse that dropping your left leg back and pressing its side means (is a cue for) "pick up your right lead." In the interim, with a young horse, you will first position it, then add speed. You will simultaneously apply your cue to teach the cue through association—but in the beginning you must set the horse up so that it "can't help but" end up in the lead you want. Instructions can be made as complicated as you can imagine, but if you keep the following in mind, you'll find this rather simple: To get your right lead, you need to position the horse with it's hind end slightly to the right, ask the horse to speed up, and cue.

There are at least a dozen ways to properly position your horse to pick up a lead. The simplest is to ask for a "lousy" side pass: For a left lead, pick up your left rein and ask the horse to move his entire body to the right, allowing the hips to slightly trail to the left, trailing the shoulders by just a bit. Keep a very slight bend in the horse's neck, bent toward the left in this case (this will help keep his shoulders correctly positioned). Squeeze evenly with both legs and kiss. If your horse stays soft and in the position you've created as it moves off, it'll pick up the correct lead. (Note that if you allow the hips to drag too much to one side, the horse will actually be positioned to pick up the wrong lead. Don't allow the hip to be offset by more than a few inches.)

Alternatively, if you've trained the horse to bring its haunches over, (that is to say "in"), you can specifically call on the hips to step to the left, apply impulsion—and pick up your left lead. Or you can ask the shoulders to step right, leaving the hips skewed to the left, apply impulsion and pick up your left lead. Or you can circle tightly to the left, apply impulsion, pick up your left lead. Or you can trot up to a fence (the fence on your left) at an angle (of about 45 degrees), then direct-rein the horse sharply back to the left along the fence, adding a kiss, cue and impulsion and take up your left lead. Anything that causes the hips to become positioned just slightly to the left of the shoulders will get you a left lead and vice versa.

Go ahead and try any of those things. Ask the horse to trot, then position the feet and body to mimic the lead you'd like to pick up. If the horse gets the correct lead, pet him, travel four beats forward, then bring him back to a trot. Calm the horse and yourself, slowly take up the reins and ask again. For twenty minutes, practice only your setups and departures. At first, you'll feel like a can a paint being mixed at the local hardware store—but he'll soon smooth out. Horses best learn to lope—and to get into the lope—by practicing their take off—not so much by traveling around in infinite circles. Yes, they gain physically from the exercise of carrying you around (learning better balance and developing lungs and muscle memory) so loping per se should have a place in your training schedule—but practicing actual departures is where you need to spend your time at the outset. The actual change from trotting to loping, the transition itself, forces the horse to consider what actions he must take to carry the both of you, the cue and what it means, the leg pattern, the shape he travels in, the timing, the balance required. It keeps his mind focused, chewing over the task at hand. What do you get when he simply runs in a circle? Ten seconds after you begin, he's thinking about his buddy in the other paddock, the gate, the barking dog or a million-and-one other things.

Note that every horse is different, bringing to the table a different mix of emotions. Some will settle down more readily when your emphasis is placed upon repeated lead departures as outlined. Others will do best when you get them into the lope and leave them there, allowing them to settle in and relax. Nothing is sacrosanct; experiment to see which training cocktail works for your rider and horse combination and move exercises around as needed.

If the horse doesn't get the correct lead, let him travel for a couple of beats before slowing back to a trot and trying again. To more strongly say "You missed my request back there," you can stop and back several steps before moving forward and trying again. Reprimanding him too harshly for picking the incorrect lead will not teach him that he got the wrong lead—it'll teach him to fear the departure. Remember, it's his positioning and relaxed body prior to "lift off" that get you the correct lead. If he continually jumps off incorrectly, go back and practice getting soft, resistance-free transitions from a stop to a walk, walk to trot, (as covered in the chapter called "Softening"). This time, add a new wrinkle: Practice your transitions, using but a single rein, asking the horse to move at an angle into the next gait, (moving diagonally), practicing both speeding up and slowing down. This will soften the horse quickly—but also teach it to position itself properly and become more animated. Be careful to get this movement with one rein, not two. (For more, refer back to the "Diagonal Movement" chapter.)

A Fix for Cross-Firing (aka "Cross-Cantering")

Q: "How do I fix cross-firing in the lope? How do I even know when it's happening?

Barbara M. in Blue Luna, MD writes:

What do I do to fix cross-firing? When I'm lungeing my horse and she cross-fires, I drop her to a trot, then ask for the lope again. When she is correct, I let her go and praise her. Is this correct?

And when I'm riding, I can't tell if she is doing it or not. Any tips on how to tell? It doesn't feel any different to me.

If you think your horse is "cross-firing," that is, he's loping on one lead in the front, another in the back, here's how to tell for sure: Go put a load of clothes into the wash. Then, during the "spin cycle," purposely move all the clothes to one side. Sit on the washing machine as you turn it back on. That wild, crazy, to-and-fro movement you feel? That's your washer "cross-firing."

("Cross-firing" is also known as "cross-cantering." One might also say that your lope or canter is "disunited.")

Your horse will feel like that washing machine when it cross-fires. While there are exceptions to every rule, every cross-firing horse I've ridden feels like that out-of-balance washer. It is unmistakable and if you "kind of think" he "might be" doing it he's probably not; he's probably just stiff and awkward (and therefore, needs softening and more practice at the canter). If you feel like your hips are being thrown violently "back and to the right then forward and to the left" (or vice versa), then my money's on "cross-firing."

How to fix it the moment it happens: Take the rein on the outside of your circle (so, the right rein if you're ambling left) and pull it back toward the horse's hip on the same side. You'll be causing that hip to move over and get back in time with the front.

How to fix this long term: If your horse does this persistently, don't turn to fast fixes repeatedly as described above. Instead, know that this happens because your horse is stiff, stem to stern, and make a concerted effort to remedy this. When you spend time teaching your horse to stay calm and relaxed through the canter, this problem will simply disappear.

Look at it this way: You're going camping. You stop at the local gas station for ice. Before putting the ice in your cooler, what's the first thing you usually do? You drop the ice on the ground to break that brick of ice (back) into separate cubes. That brick of ice was useless; it'd just sit on top of your drinks, a waste of money. By contrast, a bag of cubes can be poured out and used. Like that bag of ice, your horse's body needs to be broken (that is, softened) into its individual parts. A giant "block of a horse" isn't going to do anything fluid. Your counter-canter is proof of this.

Find exercises designed to soften up your horse both laterally (side-to-side) and vertically (up and down, nose to tail). For example, practice serpentine exercises where you ask the horse to turn to the left, holding your rein until the horse also softens his neck and/or drops his head before turning off to the right and repeating. (Refer to the chapters "Classic Serpentine" and "Softening.")

Get better with your hands. Without the proper timing and release, you'll only prompt your horse to brace against your hold each time you touch the reins. (Refer to the chapters "How to Pick Up Your Reins Like a Pro" and "Training Magic: Release on the Thought")

Improve your horse's ability to carry your weight at faster speeds in a relaxed and correct fashion by loping five strides, then trotting for five strides, then again asking for the lope. Repeat that sequence for a solid 20 minutes, minimum. Repeatedly transitioning, to and from the lope, will soon teach the horse how to prepare himself for the lope, how to carry the two of you in the lope—and to not be scared of the lope. Stay on the same lead each time, concentrating on keeping things simple. Practice the other lead in a separate 20 minute session. (Refer to the chapters "Softening" and "Getting Leads")

Finally, look for materials explaining how to "counter-canter," (as opposed to "cross-canter"), an excellent exercise designed to teach your horse improved balance, flexibility, and athleticism. (For a brief reference, consult the tail end of the chapter "The Reverse Arc Circle.")

Hips, Get Behind the Shoulders (And Stay Put)

A little exercise with big results. Teach your horse to automatically align its hips and shoulders in an arc mirroring your line of travel to improve collection and see the following: 1) Rounder circles; 2) Straighter straights; 3) Vastly improved stops. (Oh! And it cures rubber necking!)

Prerequisite: The ability to drop your horse's head and to keep it soft, not pulling or bracing on the reins. You should also be able to move your horse's hips with a single rein and to direct-rein its shoulders to the left and right. (For how-to, refer to the previous chapters "Hip Control Part I," "Clockwork," "Softening," and "Shoulder Control.")

If your horse has the habit of bringing its head over to your boot rather than turning gracefully in the direction its nose is pointed – or traveling with its hips jutted left and its shoulders cocked right, here's your long-term fix. Given enough practice, you'll teach your horse to automatically bring its hips into correct alignment behind the shoulders the moment you pick up the inside rein.* You'll get round circles, straight lines, and better braking when the horse keeps a balanced frame. (*Again, the "inside rein" is the rein you pick up first, the rein that calls the shots in your current exercise.)

Walk or trot forward and ask the horse to lower its head, to stay soft through the reins, and to bring its chin toward its chest. Next, keep the head in place and use a single rein to ask the horse to move its hips over a step or two – just a simple disengagement as you've practiced. (If you can't easily keep the head correctly situated, stop and practice just that until you can.) Note, and this is important: You want to pivot the back foot diagonally forward not simply "across." If a giant clock was lying under your horse's back leg, you'd move it toward "four," not "three" (or "eight," not "nine"). Next, use the OTHER rein, a direct rein, to bring the front leg across, onto its own "three" (or "nine"). You'll be moving the hip right, then the shoulder right and vice-versa.

Here is a specific example: 1) Use the left rein to move the back right leg onto four; 2) Keep the head properly placed; 3) Use the right (direct) rein to move the front right leg onto three. Your horse should then be standing with the hips aligned behind the shoulders. At that point, you've finished the exercise, but in the moments afterward, as you continue moving forward, actively work to keep your horse in a proper frame. You want it's forehead "on the vertical," its chin approaching its chest, in an effort to retain the "roundness" you've just created. After a moment or two, turn and practice in the opposite direction: Move the back to the left onto eight, the front to the left onto nine.

Why hips onto four but shoulders onto three? Because bringing the hips a bit forward (as happens when they step diagonally onto four o'clock as prescribed) then the shoulders across in front of the back legs, shortens the distance between the nose and the tail of the horse. The back end moves ahead but the nose stays in place – possible because the spine or topline of the horse bows upward a fraction of an inch. This is a good thing because you're effectively compressing a spring and like the spring (or a rattle snake, for that matter) that energy can be used to quickly burst forward, change direction, travel in a more lively fashion (think "more showy"), or lift smartly into a lope departure. True and lasting "collection" requires a great deal of time and practice in a multitude of exercises but this "rounding" is what it's largely about, making this exercise an excellent step in your basic training regimen. (See the chapters "Softening" and "Hips-In" for similarly-themed material.)

To see for yourself how this brings about rounder circles, straight lines and better movement in other ways, simply jut one of your hips in front of the other and walk about. Better yet, drop on to all fours and bring your rear end several inches to the right or left of your shoulders. Doubtless, you'll scramble about like an egg rolling on the floor. Bring your body into alignment and you'll move true and fluidly.

Take, for example, your stops: Solid braking requires the horse to travel in a balanced frame, no single body part off to the side or overly-tucked in. Lack of alignment introduces a weakness: Consider how easily you can tip over the toughest body builder if he was standing on one leg – now picture trying to push that same guy anywhere at all when he's ready for you standing balanced and square – it's the same idea. Any sort of imbalance or poor alignment creates an Achilles' heel that affects your ability to stop evenly and quickly. Now you've got a way to get that horse framed up for a quality stop. (Reiners, take heed.)

Rubber Neckers and Boot Biters: The next time your horse turns to stare at – or nibble on – your boot rather than turning to follow his nose, don't get mad and snatch at those reins, show it the proper stance. Just move the hips over a few degrees, swing the head around into proper alignment, and move off to practice anything you'd like. (You'll want to briefly practice something rather intensely so that the horse comes to associate noodle-necking with more work.) For example, if the head is at your left boot, the neck is way, way over-bent, correct? You just want a tiny bit of bend because it's more about relaxation than a specific angle or degree: Use the right rein to swing the hips to the left; use your left rein to bring the horse's head to the left into correct alignment. It may take time, but with repetition, he'll know the position you're looking for. He'll also realize that over-bending doesn't get him out of anything.

Hips-in (aka "Haunches-in" or "Travers")

Hips-in is strength training for your horse, a trip to the gym. It asks your horse to "more fully engage" the back inside leg and thus develop a greater ability to "round up" and carry you in a more energized and balanced frame. In turn, you get a more obedient horse that does anything that requires a sudden burst of power, better. (Like sharp turns, standing-start lope departures, pivots, and rollbacks.)

If you've ever seen a horse that turns on a dime, flows through rollbacks and makes effortless lope departures, you've seen a horse well-practiced in "lateral exercises" like "hips-in." Those exercises have produced an athlete that keeps its body "coiled like a spring," his muscles energized and ready for action.

The term "haunches-in" (aka "travers," "hips-in," and "well-la-dee-da") sounds intimidating. Those words seem to suggest some mind-bending, gravity-defying exercise that takes 12 years, a trillion-dollar horse, and an East German accent to truly master. It sounds like something the "average" horse and rider shouldn't even bother trying. Well, the good news is, it's über easy to learn and teach.

"Hips-in" can be practiced on both straightaways and circles. In simple terms, it's when the horse walks at a 30 degree angle to the fence, carrying its front end near the fence, the back end jutting slightly to the inside (or "in"). If circling in the pasture, the horse's front feet move on your chosen (primary) line of travel while the back feet are carried slightly toward the "inside" of your circle. His entire body is smoothly and evenly arched from head to tail. Because this movement requires that the horse place more weight on the inside hind leg, it strengthens the hindquarters and improves their ability to carry weight when traveling "collected." (Left to its own devices, your horse would naturally carry the greater percentage of its weight in the front, making him less maneuverable in many things we might ask him to do.)

Bear in mind that to gain real benefit from this, you must work to keep your horse relaxed and moving naturally throughout these maneuvers. Ratcheting your horse into position by cranking those reins, spurring or jerking or other such means, will only work against you; you might even harm the horse. Keeping your horse soft, calm and willing throughout this material is paramount—so if you find your horse fighting you and tensing up, back off, give it more time, come at it from a more relaxed direction.

A quick warm-up: Walk or trot your horse along a fence line. With the fence at your side, you will repeatedly pick up the rein nearest the fence and place pressure, causing the horse to turn back to the fence, as if to go back the other way. (Exactly as previously practiced when working to establish basic hip control.) Don't actually turn back the other way, but rather, the very instant that you believe the horse is committed to turning back to its left, (specifically, when the hips move over), guide the horse back onto its initial (fence-parallel) path and move off several beats before petting, pausing, and repeating the sequence. Practice this until the horse automatically brings it's hips over when you simply pick up the rein. Consciously feel for this and work to memorize the precise feeling.

Moving on to the crux of the exercise, we will work to teach the horse to bring its hips "in" to the inside of a clockwise circle. Practice this sole direction until you can pick up a rein and feel the horse bring its hips over slightly. You're not looking for a movement of more than a few inches. (Remember, the correct movement will be subtle, nothing "big.") Typically, you're looking at 45 minutes in each direction. Just reverse things later when traveling counter-clockwise.

There are just three steps:

1) Move away from the fence and walk a large circle, around 40 feet in diameter. (If you are first learning this, practice this at a walk so that you can build up the necessary muscle memory. It's a simple process—but getting the elements clear and correct—and not muddled—is very, very important.) Walk your circle to the right and pick up the inside rein (the right). Ask the neck and shoulder to bend away from that rein slightly. You're looking for a relaxation and just a very minor curve. (The shoulder will slightly "lift" away; the neck will minimally curve.) When you feel that softness, drop the rein and keep moving on your circle, allowing the horse to carry itself as it would naturally. Make sure there was zero hesitation in your horse's gait as you carried out the mini-move just described and that it stayed precisely on track. Practice until you can hold this soft, bent neck for several strides with no effect on the horse's forward movement.

2) Next, put Step 1 out of your head for a moment. Walk your circle again and do only the following: Pick up your outside rein (the left) and ask the horse to turn out of the circle and to stop exactly perpendicular to the circle, (so, a 90 degree turn). Drop your reins and allow the horse to stand there turned out for a beat. Pause long enough to hear the birds singing, the wind blowing, a car driving by, anything. A quick moment later, pick up your right rein and direct your horse back to walking on its clockwise circle.

3) A stride or two after completing Step 2, you should repeat Step 1: Ask the horse to bow ever-so-slightly his head and neck, mirroring the circle you're walking. It should be an even bow, not overbent through the neck and not a simple turn of the head. When you feel him relax, drop your rein and pet him. Keep walking your circle. Other than prescribed, do not stop moving at any time.

That's the exercise. You begin and end by asking the horse to soften though his head and neck, lifting the shoulder slightly away, bending to mirror your circle. In between, you simply ask the horse to turn perpendicular to the circle.

Practice those three pieces of the puzzle individually until they come naturally, effortlessly. Then, practice the three steps with no stopping in between each. Ask the neck to bow, drop that rein and pick up the other rein to turn the horse perpendicular to the circle, pausing only as long as it takes to drop the rein in your hand and pick up the other rein and bring the horse back onto your circle, ending with another bow of the neck. The three movements should be sewn into one seamless "dance."

Next, run those three steps together as you've been doing—but work to keep the head and neck bowed ever-so-slightly even as you pick up that next rein and ask the horse to step out perpendicular to your circle. Keep that slight bow, turn out, turn back in and walk off, traveling a step or two before finally releasing that bow in the neck. Yes, his neck should be kept slightly bowed inside while you are simultaneously asking him with the other rein to turn out.

Given the average horse and rider, it will take about forty-five minutes of this circling before the horse learns to associate the hip movement with a total release of rein pressure. What you're feeling for is that when you apply light pressure to the inside rein, then pick up the outside rein, that sequence and combination will cue the horse to subtly move his hips over while keeping his front half on its initial path. The hip movement is all you ever wanted to create, so you would drop all rein pressure when the hip moves, then move forward a few beats before repeating the sequence. Timing your release for the moment the hips move then solidifies the idea "move the hips, that's all you need to do." Once the horse has made the association, there's no reason to turn fully out of your circle unless the horse fails to move the hips. Continued practice will teach the horse to bring the hips over and to leave them there until you ask them (via your release) to return to a "normal" position.

This entire movement is an easy thing for the horse to do. There's no force and he literally "knows" what to do, so his body stays relaxed. In turn, there is a VERY slight and even bend in his body, mirroring the circle he's walking. (If he's walking clockwise, his body is faintly bent clockwise.) You can also practice this against a wall, in which case his shoulders would be traveling straight forward, his hips drawn in at about a 30 degree angle.

So, let's say you teach this thoroughly today—and next week you want to bring the horse's hips to your right (as you continue to move straight forward): All you'd have to do would be to put a very, very slight bow in the horse's neck using the right rein, then apply pressure with the left (as if "turning to the outside of your circle") and the horse's hips will move to their right. Release your pressure when the hip moves into position. (Want the hip to continue coming around? Release your pressure a beat or two later.) With practice, you'd gradually work to increase the period of time and distance over which the horse can travel with "hips-in." (If your horse grows irritated or seems to just quit trying, it might very well be a signal that you're pushing too fast.)

That's your long-term plan, to improve your horse's muscling, timing and overall ability to carry you through other maneuvers by improving his ability to do this maneuver over longer distances. Remember, it's meant to be practiced over time by its very definition. In the same way that the human body builder lifts the ten pound weight ten times today, the 12 pound weight 12 times tomorrow and eventually the 20 pound weight 20 times, you must increase your horse's workload only gradually. You don't want to be pushing around a sore and aggravated horse. Factor this sort of work into your long-term planning. Moving into the future, repeated practice of this and other "lateral" exercises will develop and strengthen your horse's ability to stay "collected up" for longer periods of time, to "more often than not" be ready to strike off and move fluidly in any direction.

Beyond the benefits of increased strength, cadence and balance, riders of all disciplines now have another tool: Reiners have a way to easily correct the hips should they slip out of a spin and a way to position that hip for a rollback. Barrel racers have a means to bring those hips around in a tighter fashion. Competitive trail riders can smoke the opposition when they smartly bring the hips-in and over to the gate or through the railroad-tie maze. When you're polished at this, try picking up a lead and see if you don't thank me when your horse neatly brings his hip over with just a hint of a request from you.

Neck Reining How-To

Teaching your horse to neck rein is simple—and here's how.

Prerequisites: This is more of a "finished-horse maneuver" so much work must be put in before attempting this material. You must have the ability to disengage the horse's hips, excellent shoulder control and mastery of the work discussed in "Train Your Horse to Travel Straight," and "Simple Steps to Power Steering."

The day you begin teaching your horse to neck rein should be at least one day AFTER you have really nailed the exercises listed in the "Prerequisites" just listed. To an extent, neck reining is really just the culmination of having learned shoulder and hip control so you'll need the tools (that is to say, the abilities) found in that material to teach it.

In the horse world, the word "cue" means something that signals the horse to do something. It doesn't "make" the horse do something, it asks. Kissing to the horse says "move"—but doesn't make it move. We cue the horse to do something (kiss, shift our weight, move our hands, etcetera), then apply "motivation" should that cue be ignored. Example: If I kiss and the horse just stands there, I squeeze (or kick) with my legs. The legs say "Don't ignore the kiss or you get the boot."

Basic stuff, I know—but it's surprising how often folks tend to get the two concepts ("asking for something" versus "making something happen") mixed up. There is a very real difference between "requesting" and "enforcing" and it's critical that we understand when to do what before going forward—especially when teaching our horses to neck rein. This is because neck reining is simply teaching your horse an "associative cue," "When I move my hand, you move your shoulders and feet." It's not: "I move my hand and pull you through a turn." To illustrate: How many times have you seen cowboys in an old movie take their hands far across the horse's mane to turn the horse? Do their horses turn? Sure they do—but due to the use of shank bits and tie-downs and pain and not because they've been trained to associate a movement of the rider's hands with a turn of direction. See the difference between asking and forcing? Were the riders in those films to remove the hardware from their horse's mouths (replacing shank with snaffle) and try riding off, they'd find the horse choosing the direction. (Those after-robbery bank getaways would look like a billiard table seconds after first break.)

A note about equipment: You can outfit your horse with a big-honkin' shank bit and get him to "neck rein" (quote-unquote) in about five seconds. This is because the very nature of a shank (or leverage) bit causes the horse to line himself up laterally stem-to-stern, that is, his tail lines up directly behind his rear, mid-section, shoulders, head and neck. The leveraged pressure caused by the bit makes this happen—and allows you to "force the horse" to turn left or right. In equestrian parlance this is called "cheating." This does not mean the horse is trained to neck rein anymore than completing a paint-by-numbers Mona Lisa makes you Leonardo da Vinci. When riding, the real artistry comes with the fluidity brought about through consistent communication, practice and partnering. To put a finer point on this: You want to take the time to really teach your horse, rather than forcing him because his movement will be more natural and thus more fluid, energetic and precise. You should also be aware that "pain" is a poor motivator. After some time, it'll take more and more of it to get the same movement. In the end, you'll save the headaches and come out ahead by taking the time to teach your horse properly. Bottom line: Teach this material with a snaffle bit.

I believe it was Sally Swift (equestrian, trainer, author and clinician) that said "Your horse knows when you blink your left eye." Well now, if that's true (and I believe it is), then our movements (our cues) can be tiny and still get big results, right? Oh, you betcha. So then, regarding our hand movements, let's keep a few things in mind: 1) Try your level best to never take your hands across the horse's mane when asking for a turn. Why? Because going across his mane transforms your hand movement from "request" to "making it happen" and don't get me started on that again. 2) Your goal is the ability to keep your hands in front of you, moving them but several inches to effect your turns—as opposed to moving them 12 or 18 inches to the left or right. Always remember, the less your hands move, the cooler you look.

So how do we get to a point where we can just move our hands a few inches and get a great and fluid turn? We get this by very, very, very consistently backing up our requests with motivation. We ask for a turn and, should the horse continue moving out straight, we apply our "Hey, you missed my request" motivator. We are consistent about this and never, never, ever allow the horse to slack off for even one instant. (Specific directions in a moment.) If you borrow $50 from Vinnie the Loan Shark—and miss his single request for repayment—he sends a motivator named "Guido the Kneebreaker" and you pay up. Furthermore, you make your payments on time from then on. Same goes for your riding: Each and every request you make must be backed up with applied motivation when and if ignored.

To actually be able to say "My horse neck reins," (and not cause fellow riders to snicker behind your back) you need a horse that "stays between the reins" AND upright through his shoulders at all times—and of course this includes through his turns. But... what untrained horses typically do is to lean or lay a shoulder against one rein or the other—especially through turns—and this ist strictly verboten, a real no-no.

To see if your horse does this, let's take a test: With Flicka outfitted in a snaffle bit, mount up and walk off. Raise your hands up, just below shoulder height and bring them about 2.5 feet apart from each other. (You'll create a triangle shape with your reins.) Using direct-reining, (pull left, go left and pull right, go right) ask your horse to make a dozen or so turns, meandering in no specific direction. Just go left, then forward a few steps, then right and so on. As you do, look down at your horse's shoulders. If his shoulders touch the reins as he turns, use the rein on the same side to ask him to stay off that rein by disengaging his back end. (Disengaging is motivation: "If you lean on the rein, I'll make you disengage. You hate disengaging, so do yourself a favor and just stay between the reins.") It's like the kids' game "Operation." Touch the shoulders to the reins and bzzzzzt, lose points. Doing this will show you whether your horse is leaning against your reins (rather than respecting them and moving away properly), it'll train your horse to stay "in the middle," and it'll show you what to be on the lookout for when "neck reining" later. If he's leaning now, he'll be guilty of it tenfold next month when neck reining. Again, a horse that neck reins properly keeps himself upright and between those reins.

At this point you need to take a page from "The Clockwork Exercise," fine-tuning your ability to get the horse to plant the leg where you ask. "Connect the rein to the foot" is how John Lyons puts it. If you'll recall from that classic exercise, there is a clock under each of the horse's hooves. Four feet, four clocks. When the horse puts a foot forward that foot is stepping on (or toward) 12 o'clock, backward is 6 and so on. In that exercise, you taught the horse to move its right front foot onto any number using the opposite (that is, indirect) rein, in this case, your left rein. You also taught your horse to move that same (right front foot) onto any number based on a request from the right (that is, direct) rein. (So both reins could cause either foot to step onto any number.) Re-practice now, specifically concentrating on numbers 2 through 5 and 7 through 11. Begin by asking the left rein to move the horse's right front foot onto the number prescribed, then vice versa, (right rein moves left front foot). Really nail that, then practice using the direct rein to get your numbers (right rein moves right foot, left rein moves left foot). If you've previously perfected the clockwork material this should be but a refresher. Finally, gradually begin using both hands simultaneously to ask for a step on a particular number—and realize how this mimics neck reining—the only difference being you're using two hands.

Now, before we sew this all together... We need to get you understanding when your horse actually turns versus when he "drifts." Quite often, we think we're turning—but folks on the ground see us just kind of drifting about. You need to learn to feel the difference: Lay a rope down on the ground, straight out in front of you. Walk that line and apply pressure to the left rein, "direct-reining" your horse into a turn to the left. The execution is child's play, I know—but you need to teach yourself what a turn feels like. Really hunt for what it feels like the very moment your horse actually turns off that line—as opposed to when he just leans or meanders. If you end up some distance from the rope, did you just sort of wander away from the line—or was there an instant in time when the horse actually turned away from it? Any step off the line to the left is a turn (in the same way that you can turn your horse at a sharp angle or a gradual angle). Memorize that feeling of the leg moving off one track and onto another. Feel for it and "muscle memorize" the difference.

When you're ready to move on: Place your reins in one hand, (y'know, as if "neck reining") and walk around asking for turn after turn by moving your hand several inches one way or the other. (Note: It's important that you practice this more often at a trot than a walk once you, the human, get the hang of it. Your horse will learn faster at a trot.) Follow this pattern: Walk x-number of steps, turn, walk x-number of steps, turn. Repeat for twenty minutes. The number of steps you walk before turning is up to you, but keep consistent and use that same number with each repetition. Take a twenty minute break, then work another twenty minutes. Concentrate and stay focused. When you first begin, you may want to try making your hand gestures more grandiose—that's fine if it works for you—but remember that your horse "will only ever be" as good as the least amount of cue you give him—so keep trying to use less signal rather than more (that is, keep your hands as still as possible, moving in only a small space a few inches in front of your belly button).

Naturally, when you first begin, your horse is going to ignore your cue, lean against the rein with his shoulder and just keep moving off without turning. Given this, be prepared: The very instant you feel him ignore your request, turn his hips to get the correct direction. That is, if you ask for a left turn and he blows you off, use the left hand to bring the hips around to their right, forcing a correct change of direction. Get that disengagement, then release your pressure, pet him, move forward, clear your head and repeat in the opposite direction.

Two tips: 1) When using your left hand and rein to disengage, your right hand must be ready, willing and able to jump in and help out and vice versa. If you're not getting your disengagements with your left hand alone, your right hand should immediately drop the rein on the right side and reach across to help pull. 2) Be very careful to not allow your horse to slow up, however slightly, after disengaging and before walking off. At all costs, you must move fluidly at all times as if a dance. If you're having an issue with the horse slowing up, try kicking harder, practice your timing, try differing rein angles. You might be holding the reins at such an exaggerated angle that the horse can't possibly keep moving. Maybe your horse has grown "used to" your kicks and you need spurs. Maybe you need to release the reins earlier or kick later. Experiment and do what it takes to flow evenly through the maneuver.

Note that it is absolutely critical you understand that when you move your hand to signal a turn, the horse either turns (within a step, maybe two) or he doesn't. He doesn't meander, shuffle or lean. He turns. It's very black and white. Recall the "walking off the rope" exercise. If you do not feel a "turn," then the horse didn't turn. Should he miss his cue, disengage on the same side, release, pet him as you walk forward, and repeat going the other way. Stay focused, objective, methodical and businesslike.

If your horse misses a turn and then performs your follow-up disengagement poorly (that is, if he lazily drops a shoulder, moves sluggishly, fails to complete the turn, etcetera), then set aside your reining training and light a fire under him. Its' energy in, energy out: Goose him forward, turn the hips left, jump him forward a few steps, turn the hips right. Pick up a quick trot and ask the shoulders to move left then right, left then right. Try loping and slowing just long enough to do half a reverse arc circle before loping back out. Mix and match things you've learned until you can see through his actions that he's awake again, then go back to your neck-reining. (When you add speed this way, don't forget that the actions still need to be correct; don't allow the horse to move poorly in a movement when trying to address poor leg work in another.)

Here's the sequence for a turn to the left: With the reins in one hand (I don't care which), ride forward and a few beats later move your hand a few inches to the left. Ask yourself if the horse moved his front left leg correspondingly to the left. If done correctly, the horse will follow his nose and step "off the line" to the left. If instead he leans against the rein and misses the turn (moving right or still forward), apply the necessary pressure on the left rein to cause the horse to disengage. ("Hey, you missed the turn.") Make sure to use both hands if necessary. (Don't allow your right hand to simply sit there—it must "swing in" to help out the left if you decide to disengage the horse.) Release your pressure, pet the horse and move forward, repeating this pattern to the right. Your brain should understand that when you disengage the hindquarters, it's the same as picking up the rear of a drifting boat and moving it over (as the hands of a clock) to cause a turn. Or think of it this way: You can look right and yet continue walking left—but if you swing your hips (lining them up with the direction you're looking), you'll be pointed in the correct direction. Walk around and try swinging your hips about—try humming something from "Cabaret" to really get in the spirit—you'll see what I mean.

And finally: Until now, we've mostly been concerned with whether the horse simply turns or not. But, as time passes, and you see that the horse has begun to associate your hand movement with a turn of his own feet, start paying stricter attention to whether his shoulders are staying between the reins, as practiced earlier when you "triangulated" your reins. Again, if he leans against a rein, just disengage him to say "Thanks, but that's not what I'm looking for." If you'll learn to trust your horse, asking for the turn instead of forcing it—and conscientiously heating things up if a turn is missed—you'll soon find your horse turning on a dime with but a slight movement of your hand.

Section II

Teaching you, the theory behind the practice

The First Thing I Do

Here's the first thing you should do with your horse today—and with any horse that's "new to you."

You have to ferret out those "one pound moments" and eradicate them like weeds. They're seeds that can grow into major disasters very quickly on the trail. If your horse "only freaks out once or twice a year but is otherwise great"—then you're fooling yourself. You're overlooking slip ups from your horse, perhaps on a daily basis, that will sooner or later get you hurt. Remember, accidents are by their very nature "things we don't expect."

If your horse went ballistic out on the trail last week... it didn't "just happen out of the blue." He's been telling you for weeks or months that he was going to lose it when enough pressure was applied and he said this every time he resisted however slightly the pull from your lead rope or reins.

If he walks ahead of you while you lead him, he's telling you that sooner or later he'll blow past you as you go through a gate or knock you on your kiester with his shoulder when something scares him bad enough.

If the muscles in his neck bulge toward you instead of relaxing when you put the bit in his mouth, he's telling you that he'll do mach sixty when he gets spooked on the trail.

Deal with these situations by doing two things: First establish a zero-tolerance policy; nip bad behavior in the bud the instant it happens. Example: If your horse inches past you as you lead, do an about-face and back that horse up. Keep him moving till he quits pushing back. (If he freezes pull on his head to pull his butt away from you. Getting those feet "unstuck" will allow you to keep backing till he lightens up.) Be adamant.

Second, get proactive. The first thing I do with any horse—and what I do each and everyday with all seven of my own horses—is to see exactly where they stand when it comes to "resistance." Luckily the test and remedy are fun.

And having fun with this is a key point. Realize that every horse has resistance tucked away somewhere. Like an Easter egg, your job is to discover it. Instead of chocolate, your reward is a safer, more pleasant ride. The calmest, coolest, bestest trained horse you have ever seen has a little pocket of resistance hidden somewhere. Ever see that great comedy "The Ref"? Dennis Leary needs a cigarette bad. When he's told that actress Judy Davis has given up smoking, he smiles and asks her where her secret stash is. Being a smoker, he knows she's got one or two hidden somewhere in the house for high-stress moments.

In a like way, your horse may be a real pleasure 99% of the time, but somewhere inside him he's got resistance tucked away for "high-stress moments."

So let's get started squashing rebellion. Approach your horse from his left (bridled, haltered, bare naked, it matters not) and place your left hand across the bridge of his nose, about six inches below his eyes. Look at the horse's neck and pick out the area where the muscle is bulging and not relaxed. Place your right index finger on that spot and pull a little (toward yourself) on the nose with your left hand. Your left hand should pull with a pressure roughly equivalent to the weight of three TV remote controls, (might as well use a standard we're all familiar with). It's important that your horse doesn't feel trapped; you're not wrestling. He should be able to pull away from your grasp.

He'll most likely pull away and when he does simply put him back into position by pulling again on the nose. (Your index finger should have stayed in place; don't allow it to fall away when your horse moves off.) Keep putting the horse back into position till he just kinda "stays put."

The instant you feel the muscle (via your index finger) relax in the slightest let the horse go completely and pet it. Repeat this simple piece of business until his neck looks and feels completely relaxed.

One of the things this accomplishes is lateral flexion. Lateral flexion is a fancy way of saying your horse bends from left to right (as opposed to vertical flexion, which is "up and down")—and it helps to know that you can't get one without the other. Underline the following in your brain: Your horse won't get "soft" vertically (drop his head, collect up, etcetera) if he isn't soft laterally. (And when I use the word "soft" I mean "relaxed.")

Perhaps you've heard this many times before, but it bears repeating: Simple movements like backing up or moving a shoulder across or whatever are not hard for your horse to do. They were born with that ability. What makes it challenging is the resistance. Your horse can no more perform a smooth side pass when the two of you are fighting than Frankenstein (with his stiff movements) can win "Dancing with the Stars."

Where does the resistance come from? Lots of places. Could be years of having his mouth yanked on (go put a spoon in your mouth and let somebody yank on it) or maybe, in the case of a young, green horse, he just resists 'cause nature has programmed him to. Try this: Walk up to somebody with your palm facing them and suggest (with your body language) that they place their palm against yours. Now push. They'll (99 out of 100 times) push back. Ask them why they did so and they'll have no idea. Your horse is the same way.

If by some strange quirk your horse's neck is completely soft and Gumby-like from the beginning, skip to the next step, which is: Apply pressure to the horse's "forehead," asking it to drop, in effect moving closer to his body. (His forehead will become more perpendicular to the ground.) When you get that, ask for the head to bend toward you again. This time place your entire right arm over the horse's neck. (His neck will be "in" your armpit.) Be careful not to place your head directly over the horse in such a way that if he came up quickly he'd bash you in the mouth. That's a good way to lose teeth. Keep your teeth. Don't get over the horse even for an instant.

Initially your horse will resist by pushing his head up in the air or by trying to pull away. Keep putting him back into position. Release any and all pressure any time you feel the horse relax, however slight. (Usually they'll just sort of "drop" below you.) Your "goal position" should be to get the horse to stand, completely relaxed, with his head and neck wrapped around your chest with your arms virtually draped over the horse.

At this point your demeanor should be relaxed, business-like, non-threatening and with an attitude that suggests "I've got all day."

You're on an Easter egg hunt, looking for pockets of hidden resistance. You know they're there—find them by progressively moving faster or by bending your horse into more "creative" positions. It takes time, but as your horse begins to relax for longer moments, hang on a bit longer. Push the envelope, so to speak.

As your horse becomes more accustomed to you hanging on him, (perhaps in moments, perhaps weeks) your attitude should begin alternating between business-like (as we've practiced so far) and that of the older sister giving the younger brother a noogie. Playful, a little rough, but not disrespectful or mean spirited.

Keep the sister-annoying-the-younger-brother theme in mind; get creative and have fun. If others in your barn don't think you've gone a tad loopy, you're not having enough fun. Jump around, hang around your horse's neck, push him around with your rear end. Spin around and sing a show tune. But use common sense here. After all, the younger sister's gonna get tossed out of the back of the car if she gets too annoying.

Caution: Only pet your horse when it's emotions go down, never when they're going up. If he gets excited and his head flares up, put your arm around his nose and apply pressure till he relaxes however slightly. Then pet. (And you may want to ratchet down your own energy level a bit.) Petting your horse "to calm him" is like saying "There, there, it's good to be scared." He doesn't have to be dead calm to get the pet, just "calmer."

Do you realize what you're doing with this exercise? You're changing your horse's first impulse (when pressured) from resistance to softness. Think about it: Hanging on his neck with your hand is no different than pulling on his mouth with a bit. It's just a bit safer, pun intended. Practice and build on this until you can jump around, move fast and "be a bit jarring" and you'll be strengthening your horse's "emotion muscle" in a controlled situation. Remember, if you want your horse to withstand 100 pounds of pressure out on the trail (when a car backfires or the other horses take off), you have to start by making him strong enough to withstand just one pound.

For those of you with scared rabbit horses, you can really build on this. As time goes by, you can create 20, 50 and 80 pound moments by finding progressively more scary places to do your work. Today, do what I described (above) in your pasture. When your horse gives like a soggy noodle, go find an "outside influence" like the local park where your horse will be a bit more amped—and practice the same there. If you begin today in your own arena (that'd be 1 pound), maybe next week or month you'll be next to the freeway (40 pounds) and a month after that you'll be walking or riding past the barking dog (80 pounds). In the example I just gave, all the steps between the freeway and the barking dog represents new numbers and places to work. The numbers, of course, are guesstimates and highly relative, but you get the idea.

Each Time You Mount Up, Do This

Here's one small thing you can do to keep your horse's attitude in check—and prevent mount-up problems from taking root.

Each time you get on your horse, get in the habit of just sitting there relaxing for half a minute or so. Drape the reins loosely around your horse's neck, one of your hands holding the reins there against his mane or withers. Slouch down and take a moment to enjoy the view. Breathe deep and listen to the birds, check out the coming sunset or plan out your next home improvement. When thirty seconds tick by, pick up the reins and ask your horse to walk off. This is especially important if you're running late or in a bad mood.

Why the pause? Because forcing yourself to "cool it" for a bit will force you into neutral and away from the "go go go" you might be feeling after rushing to the barn and tacking up. Rather than barging into things (and perhaps taking "things" out on your horse), establish a rhythm and pace for your ride that's calm, rational and thought-out. You're not simply "trying to get this over with."

And, do this because you want a horse that stands still when you ask it to stand still. Were you to routinely hop on and right away move off WITH a cue, your horse might very well recognize the pattern and begin taking off WITHOUT a cue and at a random speed. Then you've got a horse that thinks you're kidding when you ask it to stand quietly twenty minutes later, one that dances about at the most awkward times – like when you're trying to open a gate, talk to a friend, or wait for a train to cross. Far worse, the horse that walks off on his own has said very clearly that he's got some faulty brakes – and you've got a problem that threatens to grow exponentially out on the trail the next time a dog gives chase or a plastic bag blows by or a car honks. For safety's sake alone, this is not a good habit to foster.

If your horse is already in the habit of walking off as you mount up, then he's either scared (most likely of your hands and how you use your reins)—or he's disrespecting you (or both). Allowing your horse to call the shots in such a way eats away at any respect you might have gained previously and often goes from bad to worse.

The first time he tries this, you can simply back him up a few paces and give him another shot at standing still. If he doesn't learn to stand "right quick," then allow him to walk off—and work him intensely (on serpentines, side stepping, speed control—anything) for twenty full minutes before giving him the option to stand again. Make him see that standing is a better option. Also, get better with your hands. You may very well be applying pressure to his mouth (too much or at the wrong times) without realizing it. Watch yourself (or have a friend or trainer watch you). Study your pick up and release of the reins and see if you can't back off on all that pressure. (Check out the upcoming chapters for rein handling how-to.)

Here it is in a nutshell: Get on your horse and sit there for thirty seconds because it sets your overall pace and because it objectively proves that the horse is waiting for your command, not "taking over." If he moves off, work intensely for twenty minutes and give him another chance to stand. Also, make an effort to get lighter with your hands, releasing sooner.

How to Pick Up Your Reins Like a Pro

It is critical that you become practiced with your hands, your primary source of communication. This is—in detail—how to pick up, handle, and release your reins.

Want to know the quickest way to improve your training? Get better with your reins. The way you pick them up, how long you hold them, how much pressure you apply, and how you release. Horses toss their heads, get stiff through the neck and grumpy, slide in their training and just plain hate the site of the riding arena because of... your hands. When you attend one of my clinics and walk away thinking I walk on water at the end of the following day, it's because I've hammered you on the proper way to pick up and release those reins. Over and over and over because that's where we'll see the quickest improvement.

Besides improving your everyday training, there's an added benefit: Much improved safety. A lot of our riding fear (and injury) comes from not knowing "what to do if." People get scared, they panic and grab the reins. They freeze with six billion pounds of pressure on the horse's face. Frozen hands cork up all that horse energy, trap a prey animal—and beg for an explosion. Practicing the nuts and bolts of "rein handling" in the quiet of an evening, spending long enough to build a bit of "muscle memory," will go a long way to helping you out the next time you get out on the trail and your horse wigs out. For safety sake, drill this stuff into your brain until the movements become second nature. Your natural reaction will then be to keep your horse flowing, dissipating his "negative" energy. You'll also boost your confidence quicker than you can say "They billed me how much for the ambulance?"

You'll see lasting results for one simple reason: It's you that makes the change, not your horse. You don't have to concern yourself with whether your horse got up on the right side of the stall—the quality of your ride is totally in your hands, so to speak. See, without realizing it, the odds are pretty good that you've set up a "me versus you" thing with your horse. You want to turn right so you pull on the reins. The horse feels his head yanked, and doesn't make the connection "My mouth hurts, therefore I turn right." No, he resists the pressure and/or pain just as you would. You then apply more pressure, he resists more and the cycle continues until you get back to the barn, throw him back in his stall and swear off horses. Maybe a mountain bike you think.

The descriptions offered momentarily will first assume that you're using those "continuous loop reins" made famous by John Lyons and sold everywhere. (They're made out of boat cord, are about 3/4" in diameter and run continuously from the left side of the bit, up through your hands and down to the right side of the bit.) Are they absolutely necessary? No. No single piece of equipment is "make or break" with horse training. However, as with any sort of endeavor, the right tool for the job can make a huge difference. You can, for instance, knot your leather reins together and use them that way. But our training calls for us to be nimble with our reins and the knot you create will annoy the devil out of you as you try to slide the reins smoothly through your hands, lengthening or shortening them. I frequently begin clinics with several riders using my "loaner reins." They quickly find out how much easier those "looped reins" make their lives – and I rarely end a clinic without making a sale to each of those riders.

Many training exercises call for us to use primarily one hand. Simply put, you keep both hands on the reins, but one hand is "calling the shots." Notice I didn't say "one hand is doing all the work." Why? Because while "Rein A" may be doing the heavy lifting, "Rein B" needs to be ready to help out, pulling or handing back slack, for instance.

Why use primarily one hand? Because pulling back evenly on two reins often causes the horse to line up the bones in his body. Like building blocks, he's "stacked," head to tail—and with very little effort he can stay that way allllllll day. There are times when this is a good thing (a horse going for a sliding stop at the Futurity, for instance) and there are times when this is a bad thing, (a stiff horse being asked for flexion comes to mind). In a very general sense, one-handed exercises are used on greener horses, two-handed work is reserved for horses that are further along (and hence, less apt to resist).

Here's what you would do for a turn to the left: Ask your horse to move off, the reins drooped over his neck, your right hand forward, resting on top of the reins, your fingers curled around the reins. Until you build up muscle memory, begin each sequence with your left hand on your thigh. You'll soon begin to make your movements more subtle—but trust me here, forcing yourself to put a hand on a leg, the other holding the reins loosely atop your horse's mane, is a great way to break the old (that is to say, "bad") habit we have of holding the reins up high with no rest for our horse's mouth. If you're breathing, THIS MEANS YOU. This is amazingly common. It sounds like a small thing, this "hand on the leg thing," but do not overlook this; force yourself to rest the reins over your horse's neck, force yourself to place a hand on your thigh.

Pick up the reins in their center with your right hand, taking them directly toward the sky. Then without leaning forward, take hold of the left rein with your left hand, taking slack out of the reins (and hence making contact with the horse's mouth) while simultaneously lowering your right hand. From here your right hand will maintain contact with the reins, but remain relatively still and just a few inches above the horse unless called into action by his buddy, Mister Left Rein. That last passage sounds complicated but it's actually very simple. In a nutshell: Raise the reins with your right hand, grasp the left rein with your left hand and bring it toward your belly, lower your right hand.

It's a good idea to drop your legs briefly against your horse's sides as you take the rein with your left hand. Drop them against your horse's sides with a weight equivalent to two "wet towels" and then let them fall away, pulled by gravity to the sides. This is an excellent habit to get into, as it begins serving as a pre-cue that "something's coming that requires some degree of collection." If you're not in the habit of doing this now, it can be a bit annoying to get into this (good) habit—but you'll be glad you did as you advance as a rider. Note that this does not, in and of itself, "collect" your horse. It's nothing but a signal—and you'll need many other exercises for this to mean a darn thing to your horse—but, again, it's a good habit to begin as you practice this material.

Got it? The right hand lifts directly to the sky, the left hand reaches forward and pulls the left rein back toward your body, the right hand lowers.

When you take a single rein (as described) in your left hand, you should use all your fingers. Your thumb should be on top, pinky down—and you should wrap every finger around those reins like a fist. Don't leave that pinky out like you're drinking tea with the Queen or your thumb up as if hitchhiking. You'll need all the strength and dexterity each little piggy has to offer. Don't believe me? Try it a few times (with your pinky on both sides of the rein) and you'll soon find that you have much more strength when you use all five fingers. Use all five fingers all the time. Get your horse trained properly and you can go back to your funky rein-holding ways, but for now, five fingers.

The most common mistake I see: Picking up a rein and applying pressure – then dropping that rein and picking it up all over again before the horse has done what we wanted it to do. To the horse, it feels like you're jerking on his mouth. Plus, when you release at the wrong time, you convey the wrong message to your horse. ("Did he release the rein because I raised my head?") We tell the horse "Yes, that's it" when we release the reins, so force yourself to keep even pressure with the your reins once you pick them up. If you need to add a little pressure or get closer to the mouth of your horse, use your off hand to pull the rein through your "primary hand." (Use your off hand when and where necessary so that you always, always, always, keep even pressure on your horse's mouth—from the time you pick up the rein until the horse completes the maneuver and you offer a "full release.")

The next-most common mistake is leaning forward. Don't do it. It brands you as an amateur, it's dangerous, and it embarrasses your horse. If you're leaning forward, your off hand (the right one in the previous example) isn't raising the reins high enough at the start, causing you to lean in to grab. If you find that you need to hold the reins closer to the horse's mouth, simply take the reins closer to the sky with that "off hand" right from the beginning – or – use that "off hand" to pull the rein tighter through the "primary hand."

We're building muscle memory here. You gotta practice, practice, practice. You need to rehearse this "economy of movement" until it becomes second nature and then, when you get this pitter-patter down, you can get much more subtle with your hand movements. Watch an accomplished trainer and you'll see that he or she follows this sequence every time they pick up the reins because it's burned into their brains through repetition. More often than not, it's a subtle thing—but it's there, a pattern with proven results.

Whatever you do, for goodness sake don't forget to give your horse a mini-break in between each repetition of any exercise. If you keep steady pressure on the horse for twenty minutes, he's thinking he's supposed to remember twenty minutes worth of steps. Heck, can you remember the last twenty words of this paragraph? Break things down for your horse into small, simple "moments." It's "I pick up the rein and release when you put your foot there" not "I pick up the rein and release it when we walk around for twenty minutes." The best advice I can give is simply this: Each time you drop the reins, force yourself to hear something. The traffic, the wind, the chatter of a fellow rider. Focusing on another sense (hearing) sort of forces us to take a break for a few seconds; it relaxes our hands and seat and says to the horse "That's all I wanted." I do something similar in clinics when I stand in front of a rider (following a completed something-or-other) and ask them how many kids they've got, their favorite color or what they had for dinner last night. Anything to throw them (and therefore their equine friend) back into neutral for a moment.

To quickly build the proper timing that'll prevent your horse from stiffening up and bracing against your pressure, develop "hula dancer hands." For real. Spend the time and concentration it takes to develop the habit of simply pushing your reins back to your horse on your release. Do this just as a hula dancer pushes away her hands and fingers. (You've seen this if you've ever seen a hula dancer. They put their hands way out to the sides and "flow" their fingers out and away.) It's also the same movement you'd make if you were "reverse milking" a cow: Make a fist and fan your fingers straight out, one at a time, pinky first, simultaneously pushing your entire arm downward. (Your index finger, wrapped around the rein, will be the last contact you have with the rein before letting it go.) So, if you were riding and had the rein in your right hand, you'd release by fanning your pinky out, then the others, simultaneously pushing the rein downward, before finally dropping it entirely, releasing your horse.

Two-handed exercises: When your work calls for two hands working in an equal fashion, pick up the reins as follows: Once again, begin with the reins draped over the horse's neck, one hand loosely cupped over them, the other on your leg. When it comes time to pick up your reins, simply place both hands over the reins, your two thumbs nearly touching. Bring the reins up and simultaneously bring your hands directly away from each other, horizontally. The reins will run through your palms as you part your hands—and the farther one hand gets from the other, the closer your grip will be to the horse's mouth. Then bring your arms down into position (nearer your sides), conduct your exercise, and drop the reins back across your horse's neck, one hand back on your thigh. Hear the birds, think of your kids, etcetera., then repeat. Experience will quickly show you how far you need to part your hands, that is, how close you need to be to your horse's mouth for "proper execution" of your exercise. (Tip: Proper hand placement calls for your hands to remain in front of your belly button, not back by your sides, not out to the horse's sides, not across its mane.)

This has been some pretty simple stuff, right? It is—but don't underestimate the impact that improving your "economy of movement" can have. Don't overlook the tips I've included (like placing your hand on your thigh, taking mini breaks, not leaning, etcetera); it's often the little things folks are quick to dismiss that have the greatest impact. Build your muscle memory. Practice this material until it's second nature and take command when you transform into a proactive, rather than reactive rider. You'll stop balancing yourself on the reins and tugging on the horse's mouth. You'll smoothly guide your horse. You'll gain confidence and be more able to concentrate on getting your horse trained.

Training Magic: Release on the Thought

Two days from now your friends at the barn will be pointing at you excitedly, stepping from your path reverently and cooing "oooh" as they watch you ride.

Psst! Wanna see some magic? How about I make some bad habits disappear and turn you into an amazing trainer? I don't care what level you were at yesterday, tomorrow you will be looking like a horse-training whiz. I'm telling ya, you will be singularly amazed—and you're gonna love this mental trick.

First, we're gonna do an exercise to get your mind right and build up a little muscle memory. Step outside to an area where you can pick up a handful of rocks and stand about twenty-five feet from a building or solid fence. Take a rock and whip it overhand at the building, watching the rock fly hard and fast through the air, never averting your eyes until you hear the "whap" of the rock hitting the wall. Do that several more times, being careful to watch the rock actually make contact with each volley. Next, change things up by taking a rock and throwing it underhand toward the building. Do it in such a way that the rock flies lazily, far more slowly than before. While the first rock is still in the air, purposely turn your attention to the next rock and lob it as well. While it's still in the air, lob another and so on. (It's important that you turn your attention away from the first rock to a second rock as soon as you release the first. This timing is critical.) You need to remain relaxed throughout; if you find yourself spitting out rocks like you're competing in a kids' game show, then you need to step farther away from the building and slow things way, way down.

The way you threw the rock at first (waiting for it to make contact with the wall before throwing the next)—that's the way you trained yesterday. You picked up the rein and held it with conviction until you saw the horse make the move you had envisioned. You wanted a step to the right and you held the rein until his foot stepped to the right. Only after the rock hit the wall did you move on.

The way you threw the next group of rocks (lobbing one, changing your attention to another and lobbing that), that's the way you'll train tomorrow. You'll pick up the rein, release it the instant you believe the horse "has the thought" and move on to setting yourself up for your next request, trusting the horse to follow through and do his part ("step to the right") just as you trusted the rock to follow it's path and hit the wall.

How will you know when the horse "has the thought" and you can release and move on? In the same way that I would know that you were about to sidestep to the left when I see you shift your weight onto your right leg. Be vigilant as you ride and you'll start to notice a pattern in everything the horse does. What did your horse do one second before he successfully completed your last request? Did he lean or shift his weight or lift his head or bow his ribs?

Here's a small example of what you might do, asking the horse first to move a leg onto a particular spot then to pick up a lope: From a trot, pick up and place pressure on the right rein with your right hand, concentrating on—and asking for—his right foot to step directly to the right. In your mind's eye, pick a specific spot where you'd like to see that hoof land—and hold just until you feel the horse shift his weight and think there's a good chance he's "got the idea" and is setting himself up to follow through. (Releasing at that moment is akin to you "trusting the rock to follow through and sail on to hit the wall" as you turn your attention to the next rock.) The very moment he shifts his weight, release the reins and trust your horse to carry on. Turn your attention to the next task, the lope departure. You wouldn't actually move your leg back and give a cue for a lead – you would use the time to think about what you'll have to do: "Gotta get those hips moved over; they're not quite lined up." "He's stiff through the neck, I've got to soften that up." "I'll lope to that tractor over there." It's only a fraction of a second – but trusting your horse to "do his thing" while you plan the next movement, will keep all of your movements flowing. Had you held the horse until his foot actually landed on that spot – and only then turned your attention to the next task – you'd find yourself running behind, reacting rather than actively planning out and calling the shots.

Dropping the reins quickly gives you more time to plan ahead and prepare—but here are three more reasons to improve your timing:

1) The quicker you can release, the better clue the horse has as to what you were looking for. Release in three seconds and he might think you released because he stepped to the right—or—he might think it's because the bird flew away, the dog scratched himself, a cricket chirped or the other horse pooted. Release one second later instead of three, and he has far fewer choices. While "three seconds" gave him five things to

mull over – a single second might have given him one or two. Fewer choices means he'll figure things out far more quickly.

2) We pick up the reins, the horse does something, we release the reins. Simple. Except... the more things we've taught the horse, the more things that rein might mean. The horse isn't always going to know exactly which "thing" we want. Eventually it will know based on the context of the situation and your associated body language, but meanwhile, it learns what we want through trial and error. The longer we hold the reins, the more things the horse will try. If two days ago your horse learned to do "A" to get a release, it learned "B" yesterday, and "C" today, then it might very well try all those things tomorrow when you teach "D." This is a very good thing. It allows us to time our releases to tell the horse "That's it there." In time, the horse will learn to associate our subtle body language cues that come with our rein cues and discern the difference. But while it's learning, we want it to keep guessing. We keep it guessing by being quick with our release. Were we to simply hang on to those reins, the horse would think "Well, it ain't "A" or "B" or "C" – I quit."

3) Holding the horse until he actually completes "A," "B," or "C" will cause him to become heavier through maneuvers, not lighter. A rollback on a fence is a perfect example: If you ask the horse to turn into the fence—and hold him fully through the turn—he'll get dull through the turn, growing heavier on the rein, not lighter. Conversely, releasing your pressure the instant you think he's got the idea (and thus committed to the turn), will cause him to turn sharper and more fluidly. Releasing on the thought will necessarily mean you'll make more mistakes because there will be times when you think he's "got it" but then fails to complete the

turn—but you must fight the temptation to babysit. The horse must be free to complete each task in a way natural for his body—not be constrained by what the rider thinks is necessary. (An example might be for the rider to be overly concerned with "head carriage" through the move—while the horse might be in a better position to do as you ask if allowed to carry his head where the laws of physics say he should carry it.)

Start paying attention to what your horse does in the seconds before successfully completing any movement. Play that back in your mind and ask yourself what happened in the half-second preceding that correct outcome. See if you can't actually release even sooner. If you notice a sequence of four things he first does (shifts his weight, twitches a muscle, raises a shoulder, lifts your right leg), then see if you can't release when he first shifts his weight rather than waiting till you feel "your right leg" lift. To simplify things, you might also try simply releasing your pressure a very specific amount of seconds after you pick up the rein. That is, if you notice that it tends to be six seconds after you pick up the reins that he takes the step, count to four and release then. (You'll be guessing at which moment he "gets the idea" but it'll keep you objective and "on plan.") Again, you'll necessarily make mistakes with this approach, especially when first starting out because you don't yet know what his "telltale" pre-signals are, but stick with it and you'll find your training success take a giant leap forward on the very first ride.

Alright, get out there. I've given you the magic dust you can use to transform your training. First practice that rock-pitchin' exercise to get the rhythm and feel for this, then trot around, seeing if you can't release the rein when the horse signals his understanding rather than holding until he actually finishes the movement.

Of all the tips and tricks I've ever picked up, of all the techniques I've learned from first-hand knowledge, videos and books, famous-trainer clinics and my certification with John Lyons... this is the greatest training tip of them all and I can vouch for some pretty profound improvement using this voodoo that I do.

What You're Feeling For

Just as another person might reach out a hand to shake yours as you approach, a trained horse will proactively read your body language and act, never waiting for a tug on the reins.

For a quick demonstration, you'll need a halter snapped to a lead line. Hold the end of the lead and pitch the halter onto the floor, several feet away. Slowly drag the halter toward yourself and get a feel for how much pressure it takes.

Would you like your horse to turn or back up or side pass with pressure just this light? For many folks this would be a grand improvement. However... things could be better.

Hang the halter on a fence and step away, holding the lead. Pull on the lead, tipping the halter toward you. How would you like your horse to move with this lighter amount of pressure? That'd be really cool, right? It would, but things can still be better.

To see just how much better, ask a friend to hold the halter while you step a few feet away, holding the end of the lead rope (the halter and lead line still clipped together). Ask your friend to move the halter in tandem with your hand movements, actively watching and mirroring you. As you bring the lead line toward yourself, she pushes the halter toward you. As you move the lead away, she brings it toward herself. Memorize that feeling. That partnership, that dynamic give and take right there, is what you want to feel when you make any request with a rein.

And that is exactly what you will get with enough practice releasing the rein the very moment you even think the horse has the right idea. With practice, your horse will not wait for you to pull his head (however lightly), but instead he'll stay tuned in, watching, acting in concert with your requests. I include this description here of how things could be, so that you will be aware of what's possible. Knowing this will keep you working on your timing and releases until you reach this ideal.

Reins Tell Direction, Legs Tell Speed

Is your horse getting duller to your cues? Do you make a request only to have him shoot you a condescending glance and go back to what he was doing? It might be that you're burning out your cues when you use them as both a "heads-up" and motivator.

When your horse backs too slowly, do you pick up the reins and puuuuulllll him back? Unfortunately, that only makes matters worse. The reins cue the horse to back up and signal direction. Pulling harder on the reins to "make it" back faster will cause the horse to resist throughout his entire body. And, when his skeletal structure is lined up like that, he can rely on his bones for support in pushing back on you—and he's gonna win. Instead, bump with both legs to get him motivated. Alternatively, try loping him for a moment with a few quick turns of direction thrown in to put some fire in his belly, then ask for your back up again. (Refer to the chapter "Better Back-Ups" for more on building speed.)

When you ask your horse to stop, do you pull on the reins—and then pull really hard when he doesn't stop? Uh... don't. Why do you think racing jockeys hold those reins tightly and rock back and forth the way they do? Answer: It's because their weight acts as a counterweight for the horse. The horse thrusts his neck forward and along with it comes the jockey. The jockey then rocks back pulling the horse's head and neck. The two help pull each other around the track like a giant kids' toy. Don't be a counterweight. If your horse needs to be taught to stop, then you need plenty of work with a single rein. He can't brace as well against that single rein. (Refer to the previous chapters that offered guidance on hip and speed control.)

When you spin your reining horse and he drags through the motion, are you guilty of pulling his head around for more speed? Well, don't do that. You're throwing the horse completely out of any natural posture he might need to complete the spin and you're breaking the rule that states "Reins signal the direction, legs signal the speed." The reins are your steering wheel, your legs are the gas pedal. If you wanted your car to move faster through a turn, you'd apply more gas. If you wanted your car to turn more sharply, you'd turn the wheel more. Get in the habit of kissing first (your cue to speed up), then kicking with both legs if he ignores that request. (Both legs, as opposed to simply kicking a rib with that outside leg. Try poking somebody in the ribs. Which way does their body bend? If they were a horse, they'd be bending around your finger (that is to say, your spur)—and away from the direction of your spin. Keep that in mind and use two legs together to say "speed up.") Or, for more oomph through your spins, try spinning, then moving him out (forward) at a smart clip, then duck back into your spin before jumping out forward and repeating. You want to make things simple. Kicking to go faster one moment and kicking to turn five minutes later is confusing. When leg pressure always means "speed up," that's simple.

When you ask your horse to speed up on your straightaways or circles—does he immediately do so—or does he ignore you and you just keep on clucking and waving the reins about? If this is you, if you find yourself clucking more than once before the horse dutifully speeds up, then carefully begin sequencing your moves—and be mentally resolved to begin firmly backing up your requests. Remember, you don't say "trot trot trot" and likewise you shouldn't ride around saying "go go go." You ask (you cluck or kiss), then bring your legs away from his sides (saying "You missed that cluck back there—I'm going to kick if you don't speed up"), then kick till you get an increase in speed. (Alternatively, you might try an "over-under" with your reins, bat or quirt or pressing with your spurs.) It is imperative that you back up your requests, getting a "noticeable change of leg speed." This consistency is key to seeing respect and change.

From this day forward, when you're training and you feel your horse stall out and you want to stoke his engine... resist the temptation to pull harder on those reins. Instead, spend twenty minutes working your horse on any exercise or pattern you've learned—and study your actions to see if you might be guilty of this. If yes, ask yourself what would be the right thing to do in your situation? The horse is stalling out—how do I apply more steam? You can try kicking; you can try some circles at a faster gait; you can try splitting up your training into more and simpler steps. Tackling the issue head on, by factoring it into your training schedule and always remembering that "the reins mean direction, the legs mean speed" will freshen things up and take your training up a notch.

Talking Horse

Wouldn't it be cool if your horse spoke English and you could simply tell him what you were looking for when you're riding? Well, ta-da! Here's a trick to get your point across clearly, a technique that's simple and easy to remember.

The next time you ride, do this: Open your mouth and tell your horse what you'd like to see. Actually say it. Speak the words out loud: "I'm going to hold the rein until I feel you move your left hip to the right." "I'm going to release when I see your withers move directly to the right." "I'm going to ask you to speed up."

This works because you're actually talking to your own body, telling it what to prepare for. (Kinda-sorta like when pro athletes visualize a winning play.) Without realizing it, you make small changes in the way you're riding and your horse feels this. Try this simple example: Hold your arm fully outstretched and say the word "slowly" very, very slowly as you bring your hand to your head very, very quickly. Now, try the reverse, bringing your hand to your nose slowly while saying "FAST!" loudly and quickly. You might be able move fast and say "slow"—but it ain't so easy, is it? At best, it's clunky. Same thing when riding your horse: Don't be clunky. Say it first, then do it.

In a similar way, reiners hum to encourage their horses to slow down in their speed transitions because it causes the riders to sit more relaxed—and this relaxed seat cues the horse to slow. Again, the performance we see out of our horse improves drastically when we change our thought process. The rider can't help but "sit more relaxed" and the horse is given two signals: He hears the hum; he feels the rider's seat change.

It's amazing how simply changing how we think can have such an influence on our horse. For years, guru John Lyons has taught people to simplify their training by concentrating on one small spot on their horse's body and releasing the rein when that spot moves correctly. He teaches this because too often riders have been schooled on doing eighty bazillion things to accomplish any and all tasks. I've seen this myself many times when teaching an adult versus a child. The young rider will just do what you ask. The adult will spend twenty minutes figuring out how this request fits in with all the other rules he's learned. "Where does my leg go?" "Thirty degrees or forty-five?" "How do I shift my weight and when?" Yikes. Isn't it far simpler to focus on just one small spot and apply pressure to our rein, releasing it when the spot moves correctly? Once again, proof that "When you think different, you are different."

So to simplify and clarify the communication you have with your horse, actually tell it what you'd like to see the next time you ride. What will naturally occur is that small changes will take place in your body's positioning. You'll automatically and unwittingly relax a necessary muscle, tilt your pelvis this way or that or bring a leg back in a subconscious signal. (The horse will pick up on this because he's been somebody else's dinner for eons and is adept at picking up small changes of any sort, particularly at reading body language.) The cool thing is that your timing will improve and there's no memorization required. You'll automatically repeat these same small signals to your horse at the same pace each time without even thinking about it. Plus, you'll be a heck of a lot more consistent than if you tried to repeat all that "leg here, pelvis there, shift now" junk. Oh—and your horse will learn faster. Neat, huh?

See Yourself Leading When Riding

I'm going to give you a training technique you can use in the saddle, one simple change you can make today that'll make big—very cool—changes immediately. Your horse will understand your requests far more quickly and all it takes is for you to "see things differently."

The following can be used by novice riders as well as those with more experience who have found themselves "stuck in a rut." New riders will be given the advantage of establishing a more-correct foundation in their approach to training; experienced riders will have a new trick to add to their repertoire. I think you'll later agree that it's amazing how simply approaching something from a different angle, perhaps employing some type of visual or mental "trick" as proffered here, can offer such instant, positive and objective results.

Here's the crux: When riding, try seeing yourself using the reins to "lead the horse from his back."

First, understand that there's a time and place for any sort of training method or exercise you might use. Don't follow anything you hear or read robotically. What might be necessary with a young, green horse, might be hugely unnecessary with a more finished horse. (Case in point, the pressure necessary to motivate a youngster is going to be different than what you might use with a more finished horse.) Maybe it's a matter of using a different approach or maybe it's a matter of using the same technique to a greater or lesser degree. (What might work to teach one horse speed control might "jazz up" another.) Maybe some of the steps in the sequence have become unnecessary. (For instance, if you're teaching the horse to back up by first disengaging his hips—but he's learning the sequence and that entire first step is no longer required because he's understanding the result you're after.) Factor common sense into anything you learn here. Try "mixing and matching." Don't be afraid to "think out of the box." And don't be afraid to make mistakes. That's a big part of how we learn.

So, the next time you're out riding, try seeing yourself as if leading the horse from the ground through each request. If you're teaching a turn on the haunches, for example, picture yourself making that request from the ground. What would you do there? Try replicating that very movement from his back. Don't be afraid to really exaggerate your movements at first. If you want him to step his right front foot to the right, then take that right rein in your right hand and really guide him over into that spot as if on the ground. Too often we make things entirely too difficult (in our minds) while riding—when the very same thing was so simple to do five seconds ago on the ground.

Understand that the horse doesn't care where you pull from, up high, down low—it's all the same to him as long as he gains a release. The real communication here comes not from some specific new angle at which you hold the reins. Any success is a direct result of you "thinking different" and your body following through with small, unconscious changes that signal your desire to the horse. (A leg will drop back or press a different spot. Your pelvis might tilt or your weight might shift.

Etcetera.) The horse will more quickly comply because you're communicating more clearly. The "bigger than life" movements you might have begun with can be gradually pared down as the horse begins to learn. Before you know it, your hands will be making tiny movements, there in front of your belly button.

That little technique there is all about helping you concentrate. You might look a bit odd at first—but relax, you're training now, not showing. Your improved focus translates into subtle changes in your body that remain consistent between requests. (And why is consistency so important? Because your horse doesn't know "when it doesn't count.") It also helps break bad habits, create new muscle memory—and you'll find yourself using far less pressure for better results.

Perfect the First Time

If you're guilty of being a bit heavy-handed (as evidenced by a stiff-as-a-statue horse) here's a Top Five training concept that will soften your horse very quickly.

Every single time you ask your horse to do something put the thought in your head that your horse will do it perfectly. That goes for handling him on the ground, riding him in the arena, bathing him, every interaction.

Huh? What if it's the first time I've ever asked this horse to do a flying lead change or to back up or to neck rein? Logic says there ain't no way.

First, as logic will also tell you, your horse was born knowing how to do all those things, you just have to figure out a way to tell him what you want. After all, if your horse could read English—and you held a sign up in front of his nose that said "Put your left foot on the red leaf"—he'd do it nine out of ten times. The other one time would require some motivation, perhaps another sign that says "I'll keep showing you signs till you do it—and I got all day." The beauty is, those nine out of ten times? He'll move gracefully because he's not being pulled into position, he's simply "doing it."

The reason that you need to begin every exchange thinking "I know you will do this perfectly" is simple: Your brain will then cause your hands and body to ask the horse politely the first time, with the lightest of pressure—and then, should your horse not respond correctly (or at all), you can apply some motivation to help him find the answer. That is, you'd apply more rein pressure, try a different angle, adjust your timing, etcetera. When you think different, you are different and so simply changing your thoughts will make a big difference very quickly.

Once I began teaching this simple concept in my clinics, it made a dramatic difference immediately. I would first see people who were thinking "Horse, you're not going to do this; I'm going to have to force you to do this." And then they'd yank. Again and again and again.

What works exponentially better is to start with something akin to "My horse stops on a dime every time; he's the best" or "My horse can back up like greased lightening" (even when the last four hundred times he didn't), then ask your horse to stop or back up or whatever. If and when he blows through that stop or back up or whatever, you need to literally act shocked. Say out loud "I can't believe you did that. I must not have spoken clearly enough." Then find the pressure, angle, timing or motivator it takes to get a response.

Your hands and your release are everything. Any little trick you can learn to work more in concert with your horse will have a huge and positive impact. Make an effort to watch a rider that you really respect either in person, at a clinic, or on video. Especially watch the trainer's hands. Make note of when he releases and guesstimate the pressure he's using to get things done. Tell yourself "If he can do it, I can do it."

Six Easy Ways to Improve Your Training

Here find six horse training tips, each designed to simplify your training and make big changes fast.

Here find six horse training tips, each designed to simplify your training and make big changes fast.

Sometimes the best way to improve our riding isn't by learning some intricate exercise or by spending years or thousands of trainer-dollars to unravel the mysteries of some dark, mystical phenomena (such as "collection" or "throughness"), but rather by making a few small and simple corrections that can make "all the difference" in not months, weeks or years—but minutes. What follows then, are a handful of subtle changes you can make to improve your riding in short order. I'm a big believer in the concept that a "one percent improvement" each day means a one hundred percent improvement in just three months and ten days—so take heed, little changes add up to big improvements.

1) When riding, we can (or should) only work on one thing at a time. (Not per ride, but at any given moment.) Example: You want to teach your horse to move diagonally to the right, but instead of moving his shoulders away from your left rein, he turns to the left. Here's incorrect: You quit asking for "diagonal" and take a moment to steer the horse back onto your "original path." You're thinking "We'll start over." The horse is thinking "Right, left, straight, move here, move there,

make up your mind." You're confusing the devil out of your horse. Now, correct: If your horse mistakenly turns to the left, keep your pressure, and concentrate on causing those feet to move diagonally against your new path. Do not stop and reposition the horse. Know from the outset that you'll end up meandering all about the pen and allow it to happen.

2) Stop riding dead-headed and start noticing things. Study the mechanics of your horse: "When I do this, I get that" or "This is always followed by that." Save these random scraps of knowledge, compile them, chew them over, and begin consciously collecting training snippets that you can put into place maybe not today, but tomorrow or the next day. Dissect things: If you notice that your mare moves her hip sideways better to the right, than the left, then look down and ask yourself what's different between the two sides? If I made the bad side look like the good side before asking for the movement, would I have better luck? In this case, if you see that she naturally carries her shoulder more to the left (and her hip more to the right), experiment to see if this natural stance is what's making the difference. Can you improve the "off side" with lessons learned from the "good side"? Try by first asking the shoulders to move slightly to the right (to reflect the body positioning on the "good side"), then ask for the hips to move to the left. You can cut out the stutter step you've added later when the horse understands your cue, but in the meantime, you've gotten your point across by using your brain.

Tip: Thinking as described is the real difference between a professional horse trainer and the casual rider. Too many riders think "My horse is a jerk and won't pick up the correct lead." A pro diagnoses the problem: "This horse won't pick up his left lead because he won't move his hips to the left. I'll gain that control through exercises a, b and c." Learn to break things down to discern the true "limiting factor" and you'll start fixing these issues yourself.

3) Begin collecting a list in your brain of "what's more important" for any horse handling situation. How many times have you set out to teach one thing—only to have something else fall apart? Should you ignore the new problem or fall back in your training and deal with it right away? That's where experience comes in and why I'm suggesting that you build this "Compendium of What's More Important."

An example: You begin working on hip control—but the horse keeps moving slower and slower. Any energy you had is quickly disappearing. Maybe the horse just plain stops. Is it more important to keep with the task at hand ("That hip's gotta move no matter what") or to deal with the speed issue? Answer: When training your horse to do anything, (ANYTHING), your top priority is to keep something on the horse moving because you can't train a horse that isn't moving. Horses naturally slow down every time we pick up the reins. Teaching them to move through this pressure is absolutely necessary -- so movement trumps all else. In the case above, forget the hips momentarily. If the horse isn't freely moving out, back off your rein pressure and/or "goose" with your legs as necessary to get that horse moving fluidly in any direction, then return to the hips.

4) Release your pressure on the thought, not the action. Trust me here, when you're told this, you'll think, "Yeah, makes sense, okay." But sometime in the future, you'll be riding and this simple suggestion will hit you like a ton of bricks: "Holy guacamole, THAT'S what he was talking about. Genius!" As simple as it sounds,

it's really one of the greatest concepts I've come across in horse training, (thanks to Josh Lyons), it's just that important. Following faithfully this one easy rule will so simplify, galvanize and improve your training that you'll want to put a statue of me up in your room. In a nutshell, it's this: Don't hold the rein pressure till the horse actually plants his leg here or there or moves his body like this or that. Instead, release when you think the horse understands your request and is ABOUT to comply. Think of it this way: If you bat a ball at a window—when do you know it's going to break the glass? Do you wait till the glass actually hits the floor before you run? Or as the ball first touches the window? Or when you see that "If it keeps going in that direction it's going to break the window"? From now on, release the reins when you think the ball's sure to break the window. (Refer to "Training Magic: Release on the Thought" and "Perfect the First Time" for related discussions.)

There are several reasons for prescribing this: One, releasing sooner tells the horse more clearly what it is that caused the release. Less interim time means fewer things for the horse to consider: "Did I get a release because I dropped my head, because that guy scratched his nose or because that fly landed on my ear?" Two, releasing when the horse "is thinking correctly" is an easier thought process for us humans than releasing after we've gone through a checklist: "Flicka stepped correctly. Check. Flicka softened her neck. Check. I have Flicka's attention. Check. Flicka's attitude is good…" Blah, blah, blah… And, three… releasing on the thought keeps us from "picking apart" the horse's actions. I asked the foot to step there. The horse understood and did just that. But maybe the head is slightly out of alignment and I continued to hold the reins—and, in so doing, I've just muddied the waters and confused the horse. Releasing on the thought MAKES YOU keep things simple. (Try it—it makes training a whole lot more fun.)

5) Take notice of the speed control you have through your transitions. The control you have as your horse moves from a trot up and into his lope or as your horse goes from walking ahead to backing up is a telltale sign. It's a major indicator of just how much compliance and understanding you have not just at that particular moment—but it telegraphs just what's going to happen when something spooks it on the trail or when you ask for a movement in the show pen. In other words, resistance under restrained circumstances grows exponentially worse when emotions run high. The very next time you ride, test your horse. Does it lift up into the lope like butter—or does it throw its shoulder and rush things? Can you be trotting forward and get a backup with virtually no stop in between—or do you have to finagle, threaten and negotiate? For safety's sake, if for no other reason, you need to address this: If your horse takes 10 feet to stop at a trot, he'll take 40 at a lope. If the cliff comes up in 39, you're toast. Reading the signs today can save your bacon tomorrow.

Work on this. Get out there and build total control through your transitions. Take the "stop" out of your back ups. Practice for twenty minutes walking or trotting forward, then backing, working furtively to remove any trace of a "stop." For twenty minutes you're either walking forward or backward. Keep things calm and business-like. Practice moving from a walk into a trot (and later from a trot to a lope and any other combination you can think of). Ask for speed and don't allow your horse to break into the trot until his head and neck are soft, (that is, "He ain't pullin' on the reins"). Give the horse a slight release any time he softens through the reins, a total release if you get into the trot with a soft head and neck. If he wants to pull through your rein pressure, ask him to move his hips left or right. They're not crazy about moving their big ol' butts, so it's a great disincentive. Practice till your horse weighs nothing as he speeds up or down or changes direction. He doesn't lunge ahead, he doesn't pull on you, his attitude is patient. (Refer to the chapters "Diagonal Movement ('Leg Yields')" and "Softening" as well as the chapters on speed control and backing up for how-to.)

6) Today your horse might believe that you expect him to move in one of three, four or five speeds: "Walk, trot, lope, run like heck." But nature gave your horse has an infinite numbers of speeds from which to choose, just as there are infinite combinations of colors. Make it your mission to teach this precision. A trot shouldn't always mean "4 mph." It might mean 4, 14 or 6.345 if you so desire. This is a big deal. Building in unlimited speeds does more than simply give you "more gears from which to choose." It also brings about far more willingness (and hence control) from your horse. To borrow a line from "Cool Hand Luke," it goes a long way to "getting their mind right." In the same way that controlling the colt's direction in the round pen builds respect, building excellent speed control into the older horse seems to have a parallel and positive effect on the horse's brain. They go from "going through the paces," to really being in tune with their rider. (Refer to the "Speed Control" chapter for a detailed explanation of how to do this.)

Rider Checklists

Here are 3 "Rider Checklists." Together, they'll keep you safer—and accelerate your training to boot.

When we don't have an objective means of approaching our training, when we simply "ride," reacting emotionally to what's happening, we're asking for a wreck—or at the very least, a bad day. The horse gets confused and we get frustrated or lose our temper. It's not an environment conducive to a proper education.

Each of the following lists will cover small things you can simply check off in your brain. Basically, has something happened or not? If the answer is "not," I'll tell you what to do. Your answers to those questions will, flowchart-like, tell you how to act in the moment or how best to form your day's game plan.

The lists were created to "be done in order."

Checklist 1: Are We Training Today or Joy Riding?

Before you ever get on your horse, back when you're approaching the barn, ask yourself one easy question: "Am I training today or am I joyriding?" If you answer "training," skip to Checklist Two. If you answered "Uh, I'd like a day off from training, please. I got a horse to have FUN, Mr. Wet Blanket Trainer Man"—that's great, too. It's great as long as you can honestly say that not once in the last few days or months have you turned to a friend and said something akin to "Flicka nearly bucked my teeth out back there" or "This (expletive deleted) horse won't stop if it sees your horse take off. What's the number for the tiger sanctuary?" If there are known issues, especially those that might get you hurt, then it doesn't matter where you ride (trail or arena), the fact is, you need to be training as opposed to joyriding.

At clinic after clinic, here in the states or in Europe, I get a version of the same question: "I'm out on the trail. On a cliff. With a ten thousand foot drop to my right and cactus on the left. My horse hates plastic bags—but one blows by and he freaks. What do I do?" To which I answer something akin to "Say your prayers." See, training is not a widget that you carry in your back pocket and pull out like a parachute when the plane goes down. It's about practice and preparation. Ignoring warning signs and riding into potential disaster is like eating a cake every night and suddenly freaking when the scale reads "300."

If riding your horse has become an aggravation or something that—even at times—frightens you, then you gotta answer "training" until riding is fun again. Following this simple thought process will have a bigger impact than if I told you to specifically do a, b, or c—because there are trillions of horse and rider combinations and situations that might be described. So, with a nod to the ol' John Lyons axiom "Ride Where You Can, Not Where You Can't," we'll consciously pick a reasonably safe place to do our training and get at it.

Here are three scenarios where things can go from bad to worse if you don't take charge right away:

Example One: You mount up and head for the trail. You ask to turn south – but apparently your horse thinks you don't mean it and keeps heading north. If your cue to turn is ignored in the best of times, it's gonna be a nightmare on the trail when your neighbor's horse comes charging up to the fence looking for a fight. Forgo the trail that day and spend your time teaching your horse to turn precisely as you request. Start with a simple serpentine, asking yourself if the front of the horse is turning in concert with your rein cue and if the hips are squared up behind the shoulders. If not, spend practice time correcting infractions until the horse turns true, keeping its shoulders between the reins (not leaning and not "leaking" one way or the other), 99 out of 100 times. Work at this every day, creeping a few feet closer to the neighbor's fence line as common sense permits, until you've installed the control you need in more dire situations. (Refer to the chapters "Simple Steps to Power Steering" and "Train Your Horse to Travel Straight")

Example Two: You finally make it to the trail, but your horse repeatedly stops to snatch a blade of grass. This is annoying – but also a danger sign. This is a horse that's ignoring both your leg and rein cues entirely and it's gonna be a car with no brakes and no steering wheel when the local 4-H kids gallop by, their horses beckoning yours to "come play." Before you become a statistic, develop a zero-tolerance policy toward any and all disregard for your cues. Be on the lookout for resistance in the form of a horse that pulls on the reins or won't move forward when asked. In the example given, don't wait till his head's on the ground. Begin testing your control a mile before that patch of grass and keep the horse busy, busy, busy. Better yet, work back at the barn. Test constantly and the moment you feel an ounce of stiffness in the neck or a pull on those reins, ask for a turn, releasing your pressure when the horse softens its grip, (disengaging if it becomes a stand-off, the horse refusing to oblige). Do serpentines until he relaxes and agrees to play by your rules.

Same goes for the horse that doesn't instantly move in response to your kiss cue. If you cue for a trot and then just sit there, drop any prior plans and instead work on speed control. If the horse doesn't turn as you'd like, work on your steering, and so on. Be adaptable and ready to send a very clear signal that you are the boss in your little herd of two every second of every day – and you'll defend your turf. (Refer to the chapters "Legs Mean Move," "Balky Horses," "Softening" and "Classic Serpentine.")

Example Three: The horse drops to a speed you didn't ask for. That seems like a mild infraction, but ignore such a thing and maybe tomorrow the horse will sull up and stop entirely when you want to hit the trail and it wants to head back to its stall. You've gone from "too slow" to "ain't moving" and missed your opportunity for an easy fix. Waiting until the horse actually revolts to show it who's boss might get you a fight that puts you on the ground. Put the kibosh on even small infractions the second they appear. When your horse chooses a slower speed on its own, bump it until you get a "noticeable change of leg speed." (Refer to the chapters "Speed Control" and "Balky Horses")

Checklist 2: The Best Advice I Will Ever Give You

Emotion is a wonderful thing when the sensation you're experiencing is "elation"—but it's a total bummer when you're feeling "anger" or "frustration." In that respect riding can be truly feast or famine. As riders and trainers, we've got great days and we've got "blech" days. A blech day happens when we allow our emotions to creep into our training. The horse doesn't get it or just doesn't give a darn and we get angry. That's bad mojo there—because what happens is that anger causes us to let go of the reins not when the horse simply gives to pressure—but after we've "really made our point." Or to give them an extra kick after they've sped up to "really teach them not to slow down." Things go from bad to worse and we head back to the barn dejected. We spend the rest of the day depressed or wondering what we're doing with a horse in the first place.

But you can have a great day every day! A great day is any day that we make an improvement, however small, and keep our negative emotions in check. Doing so will keep you and your horse on the same page and build a positive relationship. Get busy with your training and react objectively to any roadblock your horse (or nature) might erect and you'll find yourself enjoying the heck out of riding that day.

So Checklist Two only has one question on it: Are you keeping things objective—or are you letting negative emotion creep into your reactions? Notice the word "reactions" in that last sentence. Becoming emotional puts you in a position of reacting rather than being proactive. That's a downhill slide. The horse misunderstands something and you react by jerking the reins. The horse reacts to that by bracing and stiffening up. Break this cycle: Every so often as you ride, take stock of the situation. Are you staying calm and methodical? Are you trying your level-best to break things down into their simplest form? Or are you beginning to blame the horse? Blaming the horse is a pretty good sign we're not being rational. Get off and walk around, cool out. Ask yourself if you couldn't break down your lesson even more. Then give it another shot.

The single best advice I can ever give you in the world of horse training comes into play right here: No matter what your horse (or the day) throws at you, learn to find joy in it. Short of getting kicked in the head, you've got to react to your horse's reaction by smiling and telling yourself one thing: Your horse has given you a gift; he's told you exactly what you need to work on. No more wondering "What do I do today"? He's told you. It all boils down to this: Approach your riding with "We're going to do what I want to do" and you're asking for trouble. But riding with the attitude of "Horse, what would YOU like to work on?" will keep you forever in a positive frame of mind. You will enjoy your horse's company; he will enjoy yours.

Checklist 3:
When Can I Get Medieval On Ol' Dobber?

Whether you're leading, feeding, roundpenning, riding or just hanging out at the barn, there should always be "two versions of you" out there with the horse. One of you is Dr. Jekyll the other, Mr. Hyde. Dr. Jekyll is the nice guy, the one who everybody loves, the life of the party. He's patient, easy-going, fun and kind. Still, nobody messes with him. Why? Because of his close relationship with Mr. Hyde. Mess with Jekyll and Hyde comes out of nowhere, delivering his punishment, vanishing quickly.

But when is punishment called for? Smacking your horse randomly isn't going to win you hearts and minds—and, conversely, letting poor behavior slide is a non-starter.

The answer comes from asking yourself this: "Is my horse trying?"

If your horse is getting things wrong—but is trying—then no punishment is called for. Not ever. You can't punish him even if what he's doing is wrong, wrong, wrong, again and again and again. ("Punishment" is any sort of punitive action, from adding pronounced pressure to the reins to spurring, from screaming obscenities to using a crop.) If he's trying, you keep asking until he finally stumbles upon the answer or you find another way to ask. Patience is the rule here. Your horse is teaching you to be a better trainer (because you'll find yourself motivated to search for more effective communication). Fortunately, he can only go 6 directions (up, down, left, right, etcetera) so we know he'll get the answer sooner or later if we stay consistent. Keep Dr. J locked up.

If, by contrast, you believe that your horse simply isn't trying, try "making the wrong thing uncomfortable" as Clinton Anderson likes to say. Stave off the use of crop or spur by instead making the horse work harder: Try speeding him up. Try asking for a different movement entirely, one that calls for a larger expenditure of energy such as moving his hips if he's not willing to move his shoulders. Don't get into an argument, use that big ol' brain of yours.

Finally, if your horse isn't trying, if he's just locked you out and you've tried extra motivation as outlined with few to zero results, then consciously change your persona until your horse decides to begin working with you: Become Mr. Hyde. If before, you were patient and forgiving, now you are militant, uncompromising and exacting. You don't nag; you use decisive, telling pressure on the reins when you pick them up and do everything a tad more quickly. Be strict. Be stern. Offer little-to-no benefit of the doubt. Ask for a maneuver once nicely and if you get nothing, ramp up your pressure quickly to jolt him awake and say "quit messing around." Use your spur or bat if need be (and do so in a business-like fashion). Convince the horse that he's picked up a new rider, one that expects results. The very instant you feel the horse's demeanor turn back in your favor, return to your old, tolerant, forgiving (Dr. Jeckyll) self.

Diagnosing Problems

Do you want your horse to stop doing something? Or to start doing something? Either way, the solution lies in asking yourself "What cue or cues plural is my horse ignoring?"

We equestrians often lose the trees for the forest. We say "My horse hates white trailers and won't get in them." Such a problem seems set in stone, inexplicable, perhaps lending an excuse for a problem we never solve. But it really doesn't have to be that way. The answers are often simple when we look at things objectively. That horse, for example doesn't care what color the trailer is. He would get in any trailer if he knew and respected a cue that says "Move forward." It's just as easy as that. (That's a real-life example, by the way.)

The next time you find yourself saying something like "My horse turns like garbage" or "My horse hates picking up a left lead" realize that very general descriptions like that don't do you or your horse much good. They don't say what's broken, what needs to be repaired. It's like saying "My car won't slow down." That may tell laypeople what's happening in a general sense—but a mechanic can't fix something he can't physically see and touch. He needs to diagnose specifically "Is it the rotors or the brake pads?" then fix one or the other or both. And that is how your bill will read: "Rotors and pads: $456." Not "Made your car go slow: $456."

In the example above, your horse may very well "turn like garbage." But, regardless, the solution is to realize that if your horse put its feet on a particular spot in response to your rein, then it would turn on a dime. Teach it a cue that says "Move your front left leg onto two o'clock." (Refer to the chapters "Simple Steps to Power Steering" and "The Clockwork Exercise.")

And a horse that won't pick up his left lead has got several issues. It likely needs to learn three cues: One that says "Stay soft on the bridle and through your body," one that says "Put and keep your hips over to the left" and a third that says "Respect the reins, don't push through them." (Refer to the chapters "Classic Serpentine," "Softness" and "Getting Leads.")

You need to be every bit as specific when fixing your own horse. What specific body part do you need to control? Your fix is in the answer to that question, not in general statements. There is no "Stop looking over there and whinnying" cue, for instance. There is, however, a "Drop your head" cue. (Refer to the chapter "Teach Your Horse to Lower Its Head While Standing.") Isolate the real problem, the true limiter, then put together a training program based on improvements you need to make.

*Remember, with any training you do, you must first be reasonably confident that you won't get hurt, that your horse won't get hurt—and that your horse will be calmer when you're finished than when you started. Always evaluate prospective training against those three factors. (The first two are for safety's sake, the third keeps you productive. Your horse won't remember anything if it gets overly agitated during your session.)

Books by This Author

Check out these titles from Keith Hosman

- Crow Hopper's Big Guide to Buck Stopping
- Get On Your Horse: Curing Mounting Problems
- Horse Tricks
- How to Start a Horse: Bridling to 1st Ride
- Round Penning: First Steps to Starting a Horse
- Trailer Training
- What I'd Teach Your Horse (Basic Training)
- What Is Wrong with My Horse? (Problem Solving)
- When Your Horse Rears... How to Stop It
- Your Foal: Essential Training

Available in all major formats, including:

Paperback | Kindle | Nook | Kobo | Apple | Audio

Purchase 24/7 at Horsemanship101.com/Courses

Meet the Author

Keith Hosman, John Lyons Certified Trainer

Keith Hosman lives just outside of San Antonio, Texas and divides his time between writing how-to training materials and conducting training clinics in most of these United States as well as in Germany and the Czech Republic.

Visit his flagship site horsemanship101.com for more D.I.Y. training and to find a clinic happening soon near you.

How-to articles & trainer listings: horsemanship101.com

Made in United States
Orlando, FL
09 July 2025